It's Hard to Salute
Standing In A Wall Locker

A COLLECTION
- IN THEIR OWN WORDS -

*Memories of 16 women who served in all
four branches of the military during
World War II*

Edited by Margaret P. Lutz, WAVE, 1944-46

Margaret Lutz

ORWAVE Publishing

Layout & Design by
View Publishing
P.O. Box 955, Prineville, Oregon 97754

Printed and bound in the United States of America by
Maverick Publication • Bend, Oregon

Contents

Every Branch Has a Story to Tell

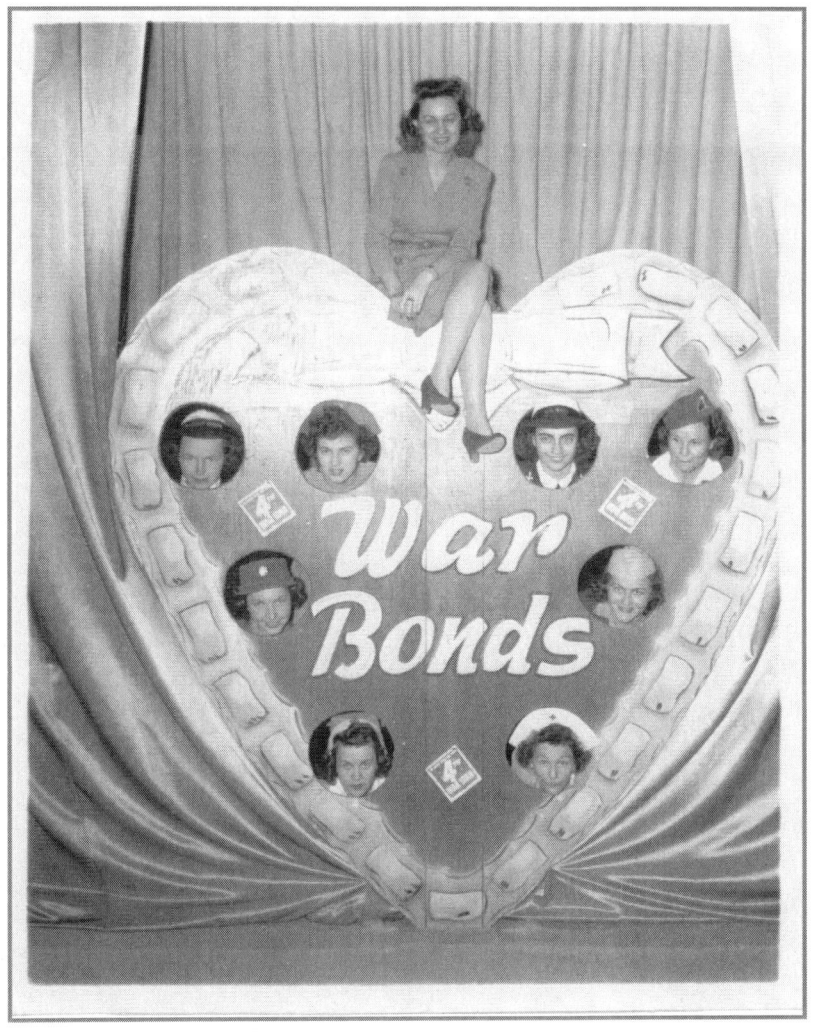

WAACs. WACs. WAVES. SPARs, MARINES,
Nurses and Cadet Nurses all served in
their respective branches of the
military during WWII

INTRODUCTION

We ladies who served in uniform during World War II have been waiting a long, long time for this book. The battles, the skirmishes, the POW tragedies, everything from dog-fights to submarines have been well documented by and about the brave men who fought that huge war. But the bookshelves have little to show for the women who donned a military uniform of their choice. We filed papers, packed parachutes, repaired fighter planes, directed military air traffic, drove jeeps, nursed the wounded, taught pilots, and a few of us even ferried bombers to where they were needed. That's just the short list. Whatever our assignment, our singular purpose was to free a man to go to the front.

No matter which branch of the service we women joined we had certain experiences in common, such as the woes of boot camp/basic training with those debilitating shots. And the off-duty times when we explored "off limits" fraternizing; the apprehension connected with being away from our protective upbringing, thus leaning on the YWCA, USO, or Traveler's Aid. Riding packed trains or buses for not just hours, but days, deprived of showers but coping, even laughing about it, BO and all!

We took our duties seriously, learning and performing on the highest plane, because like all the rest of our country-men, we were bound together in a common cause: the protection of our precious country. Sure, we had lighthearted times. Sure, we pushed the envelope occasionally, but never did we lose sight of our purpose, or the honor connected with our uniform, or our serious commitment to our branch of the service.

We are in our "golden" years now, late seventies up to late eighties. These WWII lady veterans who herein are telling their personal stories "in their own words" share a desire to leave their memories with all the underlying historical facts for younger generations to know how it really was at the early times of women in uniform. How well we took on military bearing and dedication at a time when we were needed. And ultimately, how proudly we served and now how proudly we remember!

Editing this book has been an indescribable experience. The concept actually began with one WAC, Edna Scott, telling me her story about getting caught in her wall locker after a poor decision to duck out of inspection. From there, like Topsy, the book just "growed." Each person I was referred to put me in touch with another. The stories kept flowing, twenty-three days past deadline. WAVE Mary Weatherman from North Carolina talked her WAC sister Elsie Boyer (also NC), who talked her lifelong friend Genevieve Olterzewski of New Jersey, into writing; and Mary also got her old WAVE buddy Betty Singer in Florida to participate. Betty, by the way, added current color to her contribution as she had to unplug her computer in the middle of sending it--she had to outrun Hurricane Charley in mid-August. Cadet Nurse Kay Sewell of Montana put me onto her good friend Army Nurse "Buzzy" Rukavina in Minnesota; I was thrilled to connect with WAAC Donna-Mae Smith, the Army's first woman bugler, through the Oregon VA. And so it has gone.

SPAR Marcine Richmond, WAVE Vera Hampton and MARINE Nancy Wachsnicht, all three of Oregon, and Viola Feyling SPAR in California, got in touch with me through reading my original book NEVER SALUTE WITH A BROKEN GARTER, which details my time in uniform during World War II, with all my irreverent hijinks. Others who have written here have come in the same fashion, good old networking.

It has been an incredible trip. I don't want it to end here. Ideally, readers will get inspired to call up Gramma to hear her stories; or let their old bunky know how to get the book; that possibly more and more good recall will spill out as another form of WWII history. And that above all, the stories we women who wore the uniforms have to tell will get imprinted on the legacy of those times.

IT'S HARD TO SALUTE STANDING IN A WALL LOCKER
Peggy Lutz, facilitator, coordinator, editor

Chapter One

COLOR? PUREE OF SPLIT PEA SOUP!

Edna Eglinski Scott, WAC

December 7, 1941. Our president said that the date would live in infamy and history has proved that he was correct. For me that date had a different meaning. It was my seventeenth birthday and I was just six months away from being a high school graduate. At least that was how it felt that morning. By afternoon everything had changed. The horrifying news of the Japanese attack on Pearl Harbor had broken and everyone knew that we were at war, even though the formal declaration didn't come until the next day.

I was in a study hall that Monday morning when the President made his historic speech asking Congress to approve a Declaration of War against the Empire of Japan. At the end of his words, a profound silence enveloped that large room and then several of my classmates, all young men, rose and left the room and the building. We later learned that they had gone down to a recruiting station and enlisted in the armed forces. It has been sixty-three years since that day but it is still as fresh in my mind as if it had happened yesterday. That was the beginning of a period of history that changed not only my life, but also the lives of people all over the world.

It is little wonder that I have felt so possessive of that period of our history. Since it had started on my birthday, I couldn't help but have very personal feelings about it. Over the long, tragic months and years that followed, the need to take a more active part in it grew in me until I finally reached that special birthday three years later. I was then twenty years old and though I would still need parental consent, I was finally old enough to enlist in some branch of the armed forces. My resolve had grown and become a burning need. I began the process a few months before reaching the required age, and on December 7, 1944 I was sworn in as a private in the Army of the United States. Though I was officially an Army recruit, I would not actually leave for basic training for three more weeks. January 2, 1945 was the day that I left home to begin my journey to my basic training company at Fort Des Moines, Iowa.

Now Iowa in January is not really a great place to be. It was bitterly cold, snowing and blowing. And that was the good part. During World War I Fort Des Moines was a cavalry post. The staging area where the new

WAC Edna Scott is shown above with her cousin Joe Bober.

WAC recruits would wait to be assigned to their basic training companies was actually a group of stables where the cavalry horses had once been housed. We were given old WWI overcoats which would replace more stylish civilian coats which we were instructed to send home along with the rest of our civilian clothes. The soldier who had once worn the coat I was given must have been at least six feet tall. Needless to say, it did not fit my five foot two inch frame too well. It dragged on the ground and I had to pull up several inches of sleeve before I could attempt a salute. But that coat was my uniform until I was finally issued clothing that was, if not a perfect fit, at least designed for someone approximating my size.

The week that followed was a blur of physicals, shots, aptitude tests, exercise, sore muscles, and responding to endless commands. Eventually though, it did end with an assignment and move to a basic training company.

"THROUGH THESE PORTALS PASS THE BEST DRESSED WOMEN IN THE WORLD"

These words were displayed prominently over the doorway of the supply shed at Ft. Des Moines, Iowa,where I had been assigned for basic training as a WAC private. Trembling with excitement, I entered, convinced that in this very building I would be transformed from a very ordinary civilian into a charming replica of that chic young woman on the recruiting poster.

The supply sergeant, without glancing up from her work, grunted irritably, "What can I do for you?"

"I was told to report here for uniform issue," I explained, wondering nervously if I should have saluted.

"Okay, Kid. What's you name, rank, dress and shoe size?"

She repeated my answers into an intercom on her desk, jerked her thumb toward a door at the opposite side of the room and said, "Pick up your stuff over there."

A girl emerged from deep within the bowels of that huge building, dragging a large, solidly packed barracks bag. Without a word, she handed me the rope end of the bag and walked away. Obviously the job of transporting that heavy bundle belonged exclusively to me and my muscles.

Back in the barracks, I opened that bag and received the first in a series of surprises. At the very top was a slippery pile of the nastiest khaki colored jersey that I have ever seen. On closer examination, I discovered that it was sewn into shapes vaguely resembling slips and panties. Horrified, I tossed them aside and dug deeper into the bag.

The shoes and stockings were next. There were two pairs of shoes. One pair was "sensible" oxfords and the other was a pair of ankle high beauties exactly like the ones my grandfather wore. After seeing those shoes I didn't expect much of the stockings, and I was quite right. Four pairs were of unlovely, heavy rayon and the other four pairs were of cotton which was exactly the same color as puree of split pea soup. Completely discouraged, I turned again to the bag which was still more than half full. Hours later I had tried everything on and sorted it all into two piles--those things that fit and those that did not fit. The former consisted only of pajamas, purse, neckties, hats and gloves. Staring at that crazy kaleidoscope which littered my bed, I could only assume that the Army intended to use me to scare the Germans and the Japanese into final surrender.

Again I was greeted by the grumpy "What can I do for you?" After listening to my long plaintive tale, the sergeant merely shrugged and replied, "Quit worrying, Kid. You'll fill out to fit those things soon enough." That was hardly reassuring since I was already filled out to suit me. There was nothing else to do but return to barracks, still clutching my inglorious bag full of goodies.

After several trips to the post exchange tailor shop, I finally had uniforms which were tolerable, if not inspiring. Upon reflection I realized that the sign over the supply room door referred to the civilian clothes which I had sadly packed and sent home.

Basic training is the term that the Army applies to that period of time when a happy-go-lucky civilian is transformed into an efficient segment of the overall military machine. It is also a time that is indelibly stamped into the mind and body of every raw recruit who lives through it and miraculously survives and emerges a full fledged soldier.

When I was first delivered to my basic training company I was totally unprepared for the events that would take place over the next six weeks. My basic company was divided into three platoons. Each platoon was housed in its own barracks and was under the watchful eye of the platoon sergeant, corporal and aide. That first day was spent getting acquainted with the other women in the platoon, stowing our belongings in our wall and footlockers according to strict rules, and learning to make our beds so tight that a half dollar bounced when dropped on them, and most importantly, to be certain that every person's area looked exactly like every other person's area. We were marched to the mess hall for our noon and evening meals, and finally permitted to shower and fall into our bunks, too tired to even notice that it was only nine o'clock in the evening.

The next day, which began with Reveille at 4:30 a.m. was spent doing physical training, learning to march, going to classes, visiting the mess hall and trying to remember all the information that was being thrown at us. Some of the activity was almost fun, but most of it was simply too much to absorb in so short a period of time.

When we first lined up for our positions in marching, I was not surprised to find that I was in the last line of the formation. I was, after all, only five foot two inches tall, the minimum height accepted for service women. What I didn't realize was that the pace of the marching drills was set by the tall women at the front of the platoon. As they marched along at what appeared to be a moderate pace, I was almost running to keep up with them. When the command "To the rear, march" was given, I learned very quickly that I had to interpret it as "double time, march" or risk being trampled by the marchers behind me. One other serious problem with the "To the rear, march" was the weather. January in Des Moines, Iowa is very cold. Many times the roads where we had drill instruction were covered with ice. To the eager but awkward recruit, that changed the command to "ON the rear, march"! But we and our dignities did survive and even became impressively well trained marching units.

That six-week period which seemed endless at the time was filled with so many experiences that it now seems impossible that it lasted only six weeks. We learned to GI our barracks, stand inspection, do KP, never miss mail call and still have a good time doing it.

Every Friday evening was spent scrubbing our living quarters, making sure our uniforms were neatly pressed, that everything was stowed according to regulations and our shoes were polished to near mirror gloss. During inspection, except for the ones we were wearing, our shoes were placed on our beds with the soles up, which meant the soles had to be polished, too. There was a place for everything we owned, with one exception. Many of us had electric irons to keep our uniforms well pressed, but there was no place assigned for storing irons. I learned early on that the laundry bag hanging on the end of my bunk was not a good hiding place for my iron. When the inspecting officer made her way through the barracks kicking the laundry bags, I knew I was in trouble and I was not disappointed. Her kick at my laundry bag was followed by a muted curse and I was put on report for having an unauthorized item in it. The cost of that lesson was a solid week of KP duty.

Another lesson I learned was that wall lockers are not good hiding places. One morning I was having a hard time getting myself in motion and decided that I would skip Reveille and have my bunk mate respond for me during roll call. It was a good idea but it just didn't work. Immediately after roll call when the company is usually dismissed, the Captain told the company to stand at ease and she entered the barracks. Hearing her approach, the only place I could find to hide was inside my wall locker. It was a bad decision. She came straight to it and opened the door. I can testify truthfully that IT IS IMPOSSIBLE TO SALUTE STANDING IN A WALL LOCKER. The cost of that lesson was a week confined to quarters.

But in spite of all the adventures and misadventures, the six weeks did pass and there was absolutely nothing to compare with the pride each of us felt as we stepped out in perfect formation at the parade that marked our completion of basic training. We were no longer recruits, we were soldiers and we were proud.

The stars scattered across the dark blue sky looked like flakes of dandruff on the shoulders of a blue velvet clad matron; and the moon hung like a large pearl pendant, nestled against her ample bosom.

World War II was already more than three years old and I had been in the Army for six months when I was sent to a god-forsaken base in the southern part of Texas. I am sure Texas was as unimpressed with me as I was with Texas, because the very day I arrived there it snowed for the first time in ninety years. It didn't take long, though, for Texas to learn what I already knew, that the Army was more powerful than both of us. So she abandoned her efforts to be rid of me and began to woo me with glorious spring weather. My surrender was almost complete when the fateful day arrived and my name appeared on the duty roster under the subheading "Guard Duty".

Having very little choice in the matter, I reported to the Provost Marshal's office at the designated time and discovered that I would not be standing at the main gate checking Class A passes. My assignment was to the South gate. And my watch would extend from midnight to 4:00 a.m. It was not, however, until I learned that my only companion would be a thirty-eight caliber service revolver that I began to panic. You see I was a WAC private and my experience with side arms or any other weaponry was not just very limited, it was nonexistent. But the Army, having endured many years of countless perils, was undismayed and my protests fell on deaf ears. A young corporal instructed me in the use of side arms for about twenty minutes and sent me on my way full of confidence.

That confidence crumbled into a miserable heap when I reached the South Gate. South Gate was the altogether misleading title that had been bestowed upon a ragged opening that had been cut into the barbed wire fence that marked the southern boundary of that military post. I certainly never knew then or even all these years later why that opening had been cut in the first place because it led to nothing but a dirt footpath through nothing but desert, and terminated nowhere. But this was my assigned post and I would defend it with my very life or at least with my trusty thirty-eight.

The first and then the second hours of my watch passed uneventfully. By the third hour I was so jumpy that even the brisk Texas breeze was in danger of being blasted into eternity. And then I heard it! At first, a sound so faint that I was sure I had imagined it. But no, there it was again. The rustling on the other side of the fence was still some distance away, but it was headed in my direction. Of that there could be no doubt.

Now, I am not the bravest person in the world. "Most devout coward" might more accurately describe me; but I was in the Army and, although the idea had occurred to me, I was determined not to desert my post. So I waited, telling myself that the sound was made by some animal foraging for food and not at all interested in me or in that gaping opening in the fence. But being a realist, I knew I was kidding myself. That sound was made by no animal. It was human in origin and that human was an escaped POW or some nut bent on blowing up the entire base. I stood my ground, straining to see into the darkness that loomed so threateningly before me.

Suddenly I saw a large shape coming directly at me and my last shred of composure evaporated. I raised the gun, closed my eyes, screamed and squeezed the trigger, forgetting completely that the manual stated clearly that the guard must challenge three times before firing. Not very soldierly? Maybe not. At that moment I did not feel much like a soldier.

I neither opened my eyes nor closed my mouth until a jeep slammed to a stop beside me and an MP pried the still smoking revolver from my hand. I shall never forget the tone of his voice as he muttered, "OK, Deadeye, open your eyes and look at your victim." I did, and there, reflected in the headlights of the jeep was a ball of tumbleweed. Worse yet, it wasn't even a very big ball of tumbleweed.

I wish I could say that the incident ended there but it didn't. As any recruit can tell you, the Army grapevine is second only to telegraphy for speed in communication and by roll call that same morning the story had traveled the entire base. From that day until I was discharged from the Army I was known as "Deadeye," and the "Mesquite Menace."

I did receive some small measure of satisfaction two days later when the following notice was posted: "Effective immediately all WAC personnel are relieved of guard duty and will no longer be assigned to that duty." (signed) Post Commandant.

****

As an update of my life, I worked until 1966 in the medical field as an x-ray technician, then quit to enter college as a freshman. I earned my degree in English and media specialty, became a teacher, then librarian until retirement. I was married 25 years then divorced. There were no children.

Chapter Two

CATTLE CARS TO CALLOUSES
Velma Wood Bazhenow, WAVE

How time flies. Sixty-one years ago I was a WAVE boot at Hunter College in New York. How exciting! I was the second child in a family of seven (number eight was born while I was in the Navy). I was born and raised in a rural area about thirty miles south of Peoria, Illinois. Remember the old one-room country schools? I took up a seat in one of them for eight years, then went into the big town, population of 200, for my freshman year of high school. At the end my freshman year, we moved into the really big city of Peoria with a population of 105,000. That was the first time in my life I had lived in a house with electricity and water.

It didn't take long to get used to all that bigtime stuff and I made lots of friends in my new school that fall. I graduated from Manual High School in June 1941 and went to work at Caterpillar Tractor Co. in the office. It was a large factory that made large construction machines. When Pearl Harbor was attacked the factory converted to a defense plant.

My high school friend, Helen Summerville (now deceased) and I both worked second shift, and we usually met downtown for lunch every Friday before boarding the bus to go across the river to work. In early spring of 1943 we met for lunch as usual and discussed the world situation and decided that we should be able to do more to help the War effort. Pushing a pencil just didn't seem like enough. It was then we decided to meet on Monday morning and go to the Naval Recruiting office and talk to them.

My father was too old to serve and my only brother was only eight years old, so someone had to represent our family in service. By the time we left the recruiting office, we had made up our minds that we were going to give it a try. Helen was a few pounds underweight, but was told that if she ate a lot of bananas and macaroni, by the time we took our physical in Chicago she should be up to the minimum allowed.

I had an aunt in the WAVES who had taken her boot at Hunter and was at that time a yeoman stationed in Key West, Florida. She filled me in on what I could expect at Hunter, but since I had been very disciplined my whole childhood, I had no fear of obeying orders. Helen and I gave our notice to Caterpillar that we were leaving and started planning our first train ride. When we boarded the Rock Island Rocket (the only passenger train in or out of Peoria) we were the only two headed for Chicago with enlisting on our minds.

When we arrived at Central Station we were met by Navy personnel that escorted us to the building for our physicals and the "swearing in process." There must have been a railcar full of other girls already there from Iowa, Illinois, Michigan, Wisconsin and Indiana. We all had the same thought in our head: WE ARE GOING TO WIN THIS WAR!

By dusk we were all sworn in and aboard a train. Our troop trains only traveled at night. By the time daylight was upon us, we were parked in a rail yard, but we didn't know where. All they would tell us was that our destination was New York. During the day, we were allowed to open windows and get fresh air, then as dusk approached, we were all back in our little cubby holes with the black curtains securely fastened. We traveled all night, and the clickety-clack of the wheels on the rails lulled us to sleep. Several times a night, an MP with a flashlight would come through our car to be sure everyone was tucked in tight. Our second day in a rail yard, we were backed into the rear of a troop train of Marines. The platforms of both cabooses were full all day while the two trains of recruits visited and passed the day finding out where everyone was from.

Our third night out, in the early morning, we arrived in New York and were taken from our train and shuttled off to Hunter College, the WAVE boot camp. The rest of the day and evening was spent on room assignments and being informed of the rules, etc. Four girls were assigned to each apartment. Each apartment consisted of a bedroom (with four bunk beds and four lockers), a   bathroom, and a kitchen. Surely we could stand that for six weeks or so.

We did have one good laugh among the four of us. One of the girls was from Ames, Iowa, and as soon as we were allowed to send and receive mail she wrote to her mother and told her she had been assigned "Captain of the Head" (the Navy term for bathroom). The next week, she received a letter from her mother that had an article enclosed from their local newspaper. Her mother had written the paper and was upset with them that they had not printed the fact that her daughter had already been promoted to "Captain of the Head" after such a short time in the WAVES.

Our first GI clothes were the seersucker short sleeve dresses and of course the black marching oxfords. And march they did! To chow hall, classrooms, drill practice, in fact everywhere we went, we marched! The time in boot went rapidly and when we took our test for placement, Helen and

I both got the schools we wanted: airplane mechanics. But, there was a hitch. She was sent to Memphis in the first group out and I remained at Hunter until the end of August when the next group was sent. I feel I really got the best deal as I was put in an apartment off campus with a WAVE from New York. I worked the jewelry counter in Ship's Service and the time went quite fast.

When I arrived for work one morning (I'm sure it was the hottest and most humid day of August), it was piped over the PA system for all personnel to muster at the drill field. This included the sailors who worked in the mess hall and anywhere else it was necessary to have them. The sailors were put at the front of the parade and the WAVES followed. The girls were falling like flies in the heat behind my platoon but the drill just continued. As we passed the reviewing stand and got the command "eyes right" there in the center front of the reviewing stand sat Eleanor Roosevelt. This was a surprise for all of us. The sailors were told to "fall out" after they passed the reviewing stand. They were sent back with stretchers to pick up our fallen WAVES and take them to sick bay. Later that afternoon Mrs. Roosevelt came into Ship's Service to look around the place. When she got to my counter, she came around behind it, put her hand on my shoulder and said, "You girls are doing a great job." I will never forget that moment.

About a week later, a new group was ready to go to mechanic school and I was one of them. We were going to NATTC (Naval Air Technical Training Center) in Norman, Oklahoma. Once more I boarded a troop train, however, this time we traveled day and night. We went south to Washington, D.C., then straight west to Oklahoma. As we crossed southern Illinois, I was only about 200 miles from home, but that darned train wouldn't take a right. It went straight ahead, with me on board. It took two and one half days to get to Oklahoma City. There we were met by personnel from Norman in our famous "cattle cars." They were like semis with an open trailer. The trailer had wooden benches the full length on both sides.

The trailers had roll-down, waterproof covers for

inclement weather. We rode the twenty miles to Norman and were mustered in there. Our barracks were long wooden buildings with a rec room at one end and the showers and bathroom at the other.

There were two rows of bunk beds with an aisle in between and two lockers for each set of bunks. The weather in Oklahoma at that time was much better than what we left behind. Our first day there was spent dividing us into platoons and selecting the leader of each. (Thank goodness they overlooked me on that one.) Then, of course, we were given a tour of the base and began to get settled. I had a bottom bunk and the WAVE in the upper bunk had a bad case of homesickness. It took a lot of mothering, but she finally adjusted and came out of it once we were so busy she didn't have time to think of home. Our second day was spent in formation, going from one building to another and getting acquainted with the base in general.

We were fitted and issued our working uniforms, navy blue coveralls and navy blue turbans to keep our hair away from any machinery in which it might get caught. We were also given Navy pea jackets for inclement weather and, of course, we already had our black oxfords that needed to be replaced at least once when we were in training. We had two hours of classroom instruction a day and like all service people, we had to learn to identify all planes, both the enemies' and ours. Once we started working on planes we got very dirty and greasy, so we had our own section at the chow hall.

On days when we walked out our barracks door to "fall in," if we smelled mutton cooking, at least fifty percent of us would head for Ship's Service for a hamburger instead of going to the chow hall.

There were those times on duty when we had a few good laughs at each other. Like the time I was under an SBD (Dauntless) working on a strut and another WAVE mech was in the cockpit. I heard this message "Pilot to mechanic" and was trying to figure out where it was coming from. It sounded like it was coming from the rubber hose hanging down under the pilot seat. Out of curiosity, I crawled out from under the plane and went around and up the catwalk on the wing.

Sure enough, there she was, saying "Pilot to mechanic, can you hear me?" She was talking into the pilot "relief" tube.

On Saturday nights if we had liberty, a group of us WAVES would catch the "commuter" cattle car and go into Oklahoma City to take in a show, then get a hotel room which we all shared. None of us knew when or where she got it, but when we were ready to go catch the cattle car back to the base, it was cool and we were wearing our trench coats. She (who shall still remain nameless) pulled out this pint of whiskey and tucked it in the right side of her coat above the belt. She was planning on a cocktail or two on base, I guess. Oklahoma was a dry state. Even the bootleggers had to wear badges to keep from selling to each other. As we were nearing our destination, we met three commissioned officers. When we raised our arms to salute, out fell the bottle onto the sidewalk, and broke. We didn't know what would happen, but luckily the officers returned our salutes and went on as if they hadn't even seen it. I rather felt like maybe they were concealing the same thing.

The time went very fast at Norman and on the 27th of December 1943, I had passed all my tests and to my surprise, I got a station in the Midwest, as I had asked. It was the Naval Air Station at Grosse Isle, Michigan. On the way, I spent ten days at home visiting family and getting to see a few of my old friends and co-workers. On the 4th of January 1943, I boarded that same old Rock Island Rocket for Chicago where I changed trains and spent that night in a coach car headed for Detroit. Being my first time there, I was a little bewildered, but made my way to Trenton where I had to go across a toll bridge to get to the base.

The base was on an island in the middle of the Detroit River and the toll bridge was the only access unless you wanted to "paddle your own canoe." I was taken to a beautiful, big, white building resembling a home, and assigned a bunk on the bottom floor. The yeomen's and storekeepers' quarters were on the top two floors. At that time there were only about twenty WAVE mechanics. There were ten in the first group who were already situated and working. They were a big help for the ten or twelve of us that followed.

All but the Captain's plane on the base were open cockpit Stearmans that were used to teach English service men to fly. The base was divided into two sections. The upper base contained the check crew, the engine installers, and the ones who recovered the disabled planes that had landed in the river at the end of the runway. The lower base had the fabric loft that sewed the airplane fabric into covers for the planes top side. From there you graduated to engine overhaul, which was really greasy work. It took twenty years to rid myself of the callouses on my palms acquired by gripping the wrenches.

We had a Dilbert Award, which was a large hold-down nut from the engine. The nut was strung on a copper wire to make a necklace. If anyone goofed, they had to wear it all day. I think I probably wore it the most. I always used too much torque when tightening the nuts and would wind up breaking one off. I then had to use an "easyout" to get the bolt out of the engine and start over again. It was in the engine overhaul department that I met my future husband. He was on land for the first time in four years and thought it was really bad to have women doing men's jobs. We girls would usually put an apple or orange in our jacket pocket at the chow hall to have for a snack on our break, if we were lucky enough to get one.

One morning just before muster, I heard him make a remark about the "sissies". I had played ball in my teens and had a fair arm so I threw my orange at him as hard as I could. He tried to catch it but it splattered all over his face. It got a laugh from the majority, especially the WAVES. A few days later he asked me to go to Sibley Gardens with him for dinner. This was a favorite restaurant in Trenton for those who had vehicles. I accepted. We hit it off real well and saw a lot of each other on our free time. We spent a lot of time in the rec room of the USO, a mansion on the island that the Navy had acquired and had made into a USO. He taught me to play pool and on March 17, 1944, sitting in a big windowsill at the USO, he asked me to marry him. He was a great Navy guy. I didn't make him wait and wonder. When we met he was an AMM 1/C, but was made Chief Petty Officer about a month after we married. I think he was pretty sure of himself, as he had the diamond ring in his pocket when he proposed. In June of that same year (1944) we were given a five-day leave, went home to Peoria and were married with just my Mom and Dad as witnesses. My family all thought it would never last, but it did. Five children and ten grandchildren later, he passed away. We had 42 1/2 good years together. He had been raised in an orphanage and had no family, so his family meant everything to him.

We spent that summer working top side (I had been promoted). In October we both received our orders that we were being shipped out, he to Dallas, Texas, and I to Jacksonville, Florida. We had a little garage converted to a three-room house in Trenton and spent all our time there when we had shore leave at the same time. We did not want to be split up, so I went to see Captain Delaney at sickbay and had a talk with him. He said my only chance was to get pregnant, so at least once a week he would send me to a lab in Detroit. One day he called me at home and said, "Woodie (my nickname), you are going to have twins." I thought he was kidding, and he was. He said the rabbit died and I would have to take another specimen in the next week. It was successful so I went to Dallas with my husband.

If anyone were to ask me if I ever regretted going into service, and would I do it again? I'd say "NOT AT ALL, and YOU BET!"

I am now 81 years old, have raised one daughter and four sons, two who have served in the Naval Reserves. I have 10 grandchildren, one who did 4 years in the Navy, and a granddaughter who did her stint in the Army Air Force and is now in the Naval Reserves. Just had the 6th great-grandchild in July of 2004. I was widowed in 1985. I worked for the state of Illinois in the Labor Department for 4 years; 11 ½ years in the office of a general practitioner, then retired from an eye specialist's office after 18 years.

We worked on Stearmans but never got to fly in them. Several years ago there was a bomber on display at our local airport, and a post-war pilot was there with his Stearman. My youngest son got into a conversation with him and he told the pilot, "That's the kind of plane my mother worked on in the Navy." The next day found me in the front cockpit of this very Stearman. I had a nice flight all around the area. He gave me this "Certificate" to validate the trip.

THIS IS TO CERTIFY THAT ON July 24 2002.

VELMA BAZHENOW

TOOK THEIR FIRST OPEN COCKPIT BIPLANE RIDE IN A 1941 STEARMAN PT-17 (NAVY VERSION N2S-3); ATTESTED BY:

Pilot

Chapter Three

BUT EAST TEXAS IS BEAUTIFUL!
Viola Dybdal Feyling, SPAR

I decided to join the military for several reasons, but mainly because many of my friends who had been drafted for one year didn't come home, or couldn't. And one of my brothers had been working at Pearl Harbor the morning of December 7, 1941. And I believed that women in the Armed Forces could help speed his return, also. My parents, brothers and sisters were all very encouraging. The only discouragement was from my boss who had been in WWI and claimed that no one would want to hire me when I returned home after the War!

New Spars Sworn In By EP Mayor

Civilians wore hat, too, particularly for special occasions such as the above.

Everyone was working in the war industry. All the men were working in the shipyards. Ladies were mending, sewing new things, or knitting for the soldiers. Towards the end of 1942 I was getting restless because I wasn't doing anything to "speed up" the War. I had a great job, but it just wasn't right somehow. I went to the Navy recruiting office to ask questions only. There was a terrific SPAR officer on duty who sold me on the Coast Guard. For those who don't know, the name for the SPARs is taken from the first letters of the Coast Guard motto, "Semper Paratus Always Ready" and was suggested by Dorothy Stratton who was the SPAR Commandant.

By the time I filled out all the papers it was 1943. I was sworn in on Valentine's Day. I remember that day because my Russian friend Ryia Valentine Mazen had a party and I went to it on Russian Hill after being sworn in.

I left for boot camp the early part of March. We recruits took the ferry to Oakland then caught the train for Hunter College in the Bronx, New York City. Looking out the train window to wave goodbye to my mother, I saw she had tears in her eyes. She was going to miss me! I cried all the way to Hayward -- my first taste of homesickness, and I hadn't even gotten started. On the train across the country we had a good time playing cards, singing with the soldiers from other cars on the train. After changing trains in Chicago we arrived at Grand Central Station, and I couldn't believe I was really in New York City, a whole continent away from home already.

Grand Central Station was awesome. And to see the sights of New York which had only been pictures before in my life was overwhelming. However, we didn't have much time for looking as we were herded onto a subway headed for the Bronx. After being assembled in an Armory to sit on our suitcases for much too long, we were eventually taken to our "barracks," a seven story apartment house about three blocks or so from Hunter College. I got real lucky--assigned to the 7th "deck," which meant walking up and down at least four times a day. The only time the elevator could be used was when one had the "watch."

We mustered for everything: over to the campus for meals, classes, drill and for anything extra in the evening--- down, and up again. The "smoking lamp" was lit on the 4th "deck," and sometimes I'd sit with my smoking buddies to rest my legs. The only piece of uniform we got immediately was shoes. Then it was line up for uniform fitting, shots, physicals, and class assignments. I got lucky again and had the watch Easter Sunday. Everyone else went into down-town for mass at St. Patrick's Cathedral.

Our quarters were a three room apartment with three double-deck bunks in the bedroom and living room, and one bunk in the breakfast room off the kitchen. Fourteen of us used one bathrooM--14 women getting dressed, preened and ready for the day in 30 minutes with one bathroom?

Captain's Inspection was on Saturday mornings. We got caught with the white glove on the pole holding the shower curtain. How could it get dirty with such heavy use?

One of the first letters I wrote home had parts like this: "Boy, do I feel good. I just had my first shower since leaving home. Was it perfect! Our bathroom is maroon and pink. Real cute. My watch is from 2200 to 2400 down on the quarterdeck. I'm going to be on security watch. Every hour we're supposed to go through the building and see that everything is ok.... The weather here is much like home. It was real crisp and nice this morning. Not a bit cold....we have the nicest platoon leader. She's finished her training but her school doesn't start until the middle of April so they are making use of her and a bunch of others from the First Regiment. We're the third batch to come in here...We had an impromptu pajama party last nite after taps. Our platoon had a "watch" meeting in one of the apartments ... Gosh, it's only ten o'clock and it feels like I've been up all day, practically ... Please send your first few letters airmail, anyhow--I'm just dying to know what's been going on for the last week...I have to go fix my bunk ship-shape. They gave us a pad to put on our mattresses so I have to tear the whole thing apart and start from scratch. Inspection is every Saturday morning...I guess we'll really get it then."

We drilled with some really tough Marine drill sergeants on the street adjacent to the reservoir. It may have been "not a bit cold" when we got to New York City, but when we were drilling it became quite frigid with the wind coming off what I thought was a "lake." We Californians really suffered. On rainy days we drilled in the Armory and got quite good at responding to commands to spread out all over the place then find our way back to our columns.

In the evenings we had some studying to do, but could also go over to the school building. I found myself on the staff of the small newspaper. I wrote a patriotic number called STAND BY FOR COLORS, which was featured. It also was quoted in a WAVES (Navy) book. They did put my name on it, but didn't give the SPARs the credit.

STAND BY FOR COLORS

*is heard on the morning air. Everyone snaps
To attention and a hush falls over the Campus;
A hush full of deep reverence and respect. Slowly
And majestically, the ensign unfurls with the breeze.*

*This flag represents so much to all of us...rolling green
hills in the spring....broad, flat lands of our desert states...
smoke-filled air of industrial cities...snow-capped
mountains in the distance...rushing waterfalls...giant
majestic timbers...marshy, lush greenness of the South...
stately flow of the large rivers...sparkling mountain
streams...deep blue lakes...wide sandy beaches...golden
wheat fields, dancing with the breeze...deep vari-colored
crayons.*

*"Carry on" - the order sharply given breaks the moment
caught and held in time. The spell is broken.
The uniformed figures move on.*

This was also printed in "A BOOT'S-EYE-VIEW"   WAVES

We had classes in Coast Guard history, ship recognition, swimming and PE, and march, march. I finally had liberty in New York City. A friend from San Francisco, Cliff Christensen, was in NY for awhile and we met and did some sightseeing such as St. Patrick's Cathedral, the Empire State Building, Wall Street. It was awesome. Saw the Statue of Liberty for the first time not in a picture.

The highlight of boot was the regimental review just before being shipped out. We were the third company of SPARs at Hunter. The first company of women Marines was reviewed at this time. There was also a WAVE company and a "Ship's Company." We were reviewed by Mayor LaGuardia, Eleanor Roosevelt and Madame Chiang Kai Chek along with Navy, Coast Guard and Marine officers. As we passed by them with "eyes right," Semper Paratus was being played by the band. We were all crying. Since I was at the short end of the line, I could see all the way to Spree at the tall end, and I know she was, too. A couple of months later the SPARs boot camp was moved to the Biltmore Hotel in West Palm Beach, Florida. The recruiting brochure described it in this way: "As an enlisted SPAR you will receive one month of recruit training at the Coast Guard Women's Reserve Recruit Training School at Palm Beach, Florida--a pleasant summer and winter resort." Why had I been so eager, so early? The Marines went to Camp LeJeune in North Carolina.

I acquired the nickname of "Dyb" or "Dybbie" which I am sure every one of the Dybdals has been called at one time or another. We were called by our last names only. It was time to check the duty list and I found my name on the roster for Washington, D.C. However, at the last minute my orders were changed to New Orleans (8th Naval District) as a recruiter.

Six of us, including Spree, were on our way to the New Orleans recruiting office to find women to replace men for sea duty to shorten the war. We arrived in New Orleans on a Saturday at midnight in full winter uniform, wearing our overcoats rather than packing them. (We'd needed them in NY) As we stepped off the air conditioned train we were hit by this wall of humid air and turbulence. We experienced our first "sweaty" feeling, not to be the last, as well as the party atmosphere of New Orleans. We were taken to the St. Charles Hotel and were all billeted in one large room. The St. Charles was "home" until we went out on our first recruiting trip to Mississippi.

While in New Orleans we met our CO's, set up posters and brochures at department stores, had a lot of publicity pictures taken and visited several Coast Guard installations. We worked out of the recruiting office on Baronne Street, just off Canal. Every morning we grabbed an "icy" coke instead of hot coffee. We were fitted for our seersucker summer uniforms immediately, and life became a little more bearable. While we waited for them we didn't have to wear our jackets except in the evenings.

After a couple of weeks we were split into three groups to go out into Mississippi with some Navy recruiters. They did all the advance preparations and each group had about three cities to cover. One of the Navy men was a professor at "Ol' Miss" in Oxford. We didn't get up there but stayed in Columbus, and also covered Granada and Tupelo. They'd

take us out and leave a couple of us at a local drug store with posters and brochures and applications. We'd talk to the young girls and answer questions and occasionally get a "live one." We spoke at Rotary, Kiwanis, Town Hall meetings and on the radio in some of the towns.

We were back in New Orleans for a couple of weeks, taking short trips up to Baton Rouge and other Louisiana communities. Then the Coast Guard took over the SPAR recruiting. We had three mobile recruiting units which were fitted out as offices. Some SPAR officers were sent down to head up three groups consisting of a male driver and four SPARs plus an officer. Elfie, Natalie Jones and another SPAR and I were in the same group which went to Greenwood, Greenville, Yazoo City, and Kosciusko, Mississippi. We had a blast.

In Greenville we were near the Mississippi River. The Coast Guard had a station nearby. Because they had been helpful to the locals during some floods, we were all invited to a plantation for the weekend. It was a beautiful, spacious home with large, airy, high-ceilinged rooms. We had fried chicken and all the trimmings for dinner on the screened porch with a smiling "Mammy" doing the serving. Breakfast included biscuits and gravy, or honey. We watched the field hands chopping cotton, and really experienced some "old Southern hospitality."Back in New Orleans we were issued "S&Q" (subsistence and quarters) so another SPAR and I found a room in a rooming house which had a fancy cornstalk fence across the front yard. It also had the biggest cockroach on our mantel that I had ever seen. At the bar at St. Charles I met a darling young Bostonian Navy ensign who was part of the crew of an LST heading for Italy. Once I borrowed a dress for a date at the amusement park at Lake Pontchartrain. We took the street car home and automatically walked to the back seats. We got some dirty looks from the people back there. We had "trespassed" into the Jim Crow section. Every place I went all over the South I saw signs at entrances, water fountains and restrooms which read "White Only". We Yankees and Westerners had a lot to learn. I corresponded with the ensign and received a "Dear Jane" wedding announcement at the end of the War.

My next assignment was Birmingham where we set up an office in the downtown in a street level store front. The display window was painted with a porthole and US COAST GUARD RECRUITING OFFICE in large lettering around it. Alabama is a beautiful state because of the amount of rain they get. The trees are a luscious green and the soil a beautiful red. One evening we sneaked over the border into Georgia to get the signature of a recruit's father. He worked at a small sawmill, but going through the pine trees to get there, it felt like we were revenuers sneaking up on a still.

Four of us enlisted gals lived in an apartment near the Vulcan Statue and one night when we were feeling silly (as in slightly sloshed) we ended our evening splashing around in the fountain at the foot of the statue. Our dear old maid Southern belle school teacher ensign from Georgia never knew!

We all decided to do our patriotic duty and donate blood. We were ALL turned down for being anemic! Decided our cooking left something to be desired. All I remember about our domesticity was cleaning on Saturdays, which included defrosting the refrigerator. That was the heavenly job because it was so darned hot there.

In September of that year I had my first leave. I went home and we celebrated my 23rd birthday the night before a family wedding. At the wedding I wore my white uniform because my dear ensign had said we had to be "in uniform at all times"...war time, you know. Found out later I could have worn a bridesmaid's dress. Did get to wear the bride's gown when I became Mrs. Feyling, however.

Then it was back to Birmingham for a while. We went to USO dances a lot...had to meet the girls, you know. It was fun identifying the home states of the servicemen by their accents. We also observed Italian prisoners of war at a camp outside of town. We stopped in at a radio station in Montgomery to do some PR the day the Italians surrendered. Got the news hot off the wire. The natives were puzzled about my point of origin. I surely wasn't a Southerner and didn't sound like a "Damn Yankee" either.

I was sent to Mobile on temporary duty while one of the gals was on leave. The other SPAR had been part of our B'ham family for awhile. They had one of the mobile units parked in the town square. We caught a lot of curiosity seekers poking their heads in to see what we looked like. We also "caught" some young Coast Guardsmen off a cutter en route to the Pacific. We went dancing with them, and their officers also checked us out. They invited us aboard the cutter for lunch at "officer's mess." Some of those same officers came through my office in San Francisco at the end of the War!

Before Christmas I received orders for Abilene, Texas. I was to be in charge of the recruiting office there. Not replacing a man for duty, but rather a couple of SPARs who were being a bit too friendly with the officers from the Army base nearby. So it was off on another crowded train, scheduled for a change in Memphis. We got there on time, but only as far as the switching yard. We watched our connecting train leave without us. I checked in with the Travelers Aid and was sent with a couple of other service personnel to a large "Y" where we were housed for the night. This meant I arrived in Abilene in the wee hours of the morning.

Our office in Abilene was in the Post Office building.

We had a room in a private home out of town a ways. Had to take a bus in to work. Winter mornings were cold. I saw my first icicles forming and couldn't wait to get into the restaurant for breakfast where the coffee was hot and even the grits tasted good. The little family we lived with consisted of a young Texas couple with a darling five-year-old girl. Occasionally they invited us to eat with them. We dated soldiers from the bases, usually in a group.

My first Christmas away from home looked pretty grim. Both gals went home and even our little family went to Dallas. There was a couple in the other duplex (he was stationed at the base) who took me under their wing. We had Christmas Eve and Day together and they took me to a huge square dance out at Anson. It was a traditional event and dancers from all over West Texas came. I was very impressed. One of our favorite little towns was Rising Star where they had a great little café where the food was delicious. We also went to Sweetwater, San Angelo and Big Spring. West Texas is so big, and barren. One butte on the horizon, followed by another when you passed that one. The locals kept telling us, "But East Texas is BEAUTIFUL!" They were right.

We weren't having much luck in Abilene so the office was closed. I was sent to El Paso. I think I was second or first class yeoman by then. There were two other SPARs in the office which was in the Custom House. Navy Intelligence was down the hall and those fellows were like brothers to me. I had a room in a private home of a relative of Sam Houston (so she said). My room was just off the hallway, next to the glamorous blond daughter's room. Everything was fine until they rented my room to a couple, and moved me out to the porch where I had to climb over a windowsill to get into my room. That didn't last long. I was in a new home fast. The sister of one of the Navy men took me in. She was a sweetheart. Learned how to drink tequila with lime and salt in a corner bar.

The two SPARs I worked with were real characters. Our Saturday routine was lunch at a Mexican café near the border to Juarez where a little lady made corn tortillas. In the evening we'd all go over to a night club with a large dance floor. They imported entertainment from Mexico City, but when they couldn't make it, the band would play "Rhapsody in Blue." It always triggers Juarez memories when I hear it. They had some great singing and dancing groups performing and we had lots of fun evenings there. Also went out of town a ways to a honky tonk where I learned to do "Put Your Little Foot". The Navy men were always around, so we were "protected".

I lived near Five Points where there was a bowling alley. Met some nice soldiers from Fort Bliss who took me there. Our "outside" of town trips were to Pecos, Alpine and Marfa. We'd head out of town along the Rio Grande. It was interesting to see the effects of irrigation. One side of the road was barren while the other, which was irrigated, had flowering fruit trees and green fields. This was really wide open country and the towns were small.

There was an Army base at Pecos, and the Special Service officers were crazy. It was always fun to get there and see what they were doing to break the monotony. Once when we arrived, the office was full of what looked like confetti. It turned out to be the circles left from punching holes in paper. Things were dull, so they staged an impromptu New Year's Eve celebration complete with "confetti." We went to the USO dances there because that's where the recruits were to be found.

As recruiting needs lessened, the office in El Paso was closed down, and I was headed back to New Orleans. Once again I had to find my own housing, a room in a private home out in the Garden district. The landlady was very nice. I shared a bathroom with a man in some branch of the service but I never saw him. I was now assigned to the Operations Office at the Custom House on Canal Street. We were decommissioning the small boats which the Coast Guard had taken over. There were a lot of these 38-footers, and after they were inventoried I had to type up files on each individual boat. This was in the days of carbon paper and I would be making 8 to 10 copies, listing that many boats, as the inventories were similar. Erasing errors was a pain!

I had been taking yeoman correspondence courses and eventually had my time in to qualify to make chief. I was encouraged by the Operations Officer to apply and took the tests, written and oral, and made it. My two crazy bosses took me out on the town. By now I was working with a lieutenant who went out inspecting the Aids to Navigation (buoys, lights, etc) on the Inland Waterway. He'd go out for several days, come back and dictate for a couple of days, then off he'd go and I would type what he had dictated. He was a lawyer from Corpus Christi.

I was living at the end of Canal Street on VE Day. Natalie, my roommate and I were on the streetcar coming home from splurging on a manicure when the news was broadcast. We jumped off the streetcar and grabbed a cab for home. What a wonderful feeling! On VJ Day we ended up in someone's inner courtyard and were up all night. Little fuzzy about some of it.

By now I was the first Chief Yeoman in the 8th Naval District. But the title wasn't very helpful when it was time to get out. We received "points" for the time served, and I had accumulated enough to get out but they were keeping chiefs around, so I was stuck. I finally received orders, however, to San Francisco. I was going home! No more of this driving or taking a train one more time across Texas! However, my flight home was via Ft. Worth on a very rainy night, and the connecting flight didn't make it. One more time with missed connections, this time sitting around in the airport at Dallas/Ft. Worth.

When I took the fancy train to Chicago, with a stateroom even, I had the whole day in Chicago before making my connection to the west coast. I found a USO for a shower, and then visited Marshall Field. What a store that was! Didn't know about my future in-laws so spent a long day wandering around and sitting in the train station.

Once billeted in San Francisco, I was in charge of the "Civil Readjustment for Officers" office. Had a crazy Lieutenant boss who was back from the Pacific. Several of the officers I had met in Mobile, and whose cutter we had visited, came through our office after a busy time in the Pacific, so it was old home week. Jack Rosenberg (the newspaper columnist) was in our PR office and I had some interesting conversations with him.

My day of separation from the service finally arrived. On December 15, 1945 I "got out." I planned an open house for the personnel with whom I worked. What a surprise when I answered the doorbell the day of the party and there stood one of my buddies, Spree, yelling "Dybbie!" We planned a ski vacation to celebrate our freedom.

During that last year (1945) I had corresponded with a fellow in the Navy (among others) who had met my family in San Francisco on his way to the Pacific. He had met my brother and sister-in-law at Christmas time. Since I was the one away from the family home, he started writing. I met him in February 1946 and we were married the following August. The military has always been a family in and of itself, and it has always been responsible for creating families, also, as it did with the Feylings.

****

I've lived in southern California about 55 years, but think the Bay Area is the best because I was born there! I am a widow, having been married exactly 52 years when my husband, a native of Norway--a proud American--passed away. He served in the US Navy as a Chief Machinist Mate on a repair ship in the Pacific. We had no children. I have been employed in a variety of office work, mostly non-profit organizations such as the American Red Cross, Girl Scouts, church office management for about 30 years where I now do volunteering. My SPAR buddy Spree and I have remained friends over the 50 years. We attended the 50 Year Memorial celebration in Washington D.C. together this year.

Chapter Four

I Smelled Your Perfume On My Bed

Florene E. (Buzzy) Rukavina   Army Nurse

I graduated from St. Elizabeth Mercy Hospital in Hutchinson, Kansas in 1939. After becoming a registered nurse, I and several of my fellow nurses moved to Chicago to work at Mercy Hospital. It was a huge hospital, much larger than St. Elizabeth's.

I had been in Chicago for three years when Pearl Harbor was bombed. The 108th General Hospital from Loyola University was activated and many of the nurses from Mercy Hospital joined that unit.

I returned home to Kansas until we were called to go to La Garde General Hospital in New Orleans, where we were activated. There was not enough room at La Garde Hospital for all of those called up, so a few of us were sent on to Gulfport, Mississippi, to serve in the Air Force hospital there. The date was early 1943.

I got the nickname "Buzzy" when a group of us were having dinner one evening. As I mentioned, I was from Kansas which was a dry state at the time. I was drinking a highball or something and at one point said, "Gee, I feel buzzy." That became my nickname which stuck with me all through my time in the service. We were often invited to parties at the Navy base in Gulfport. We worked hard and enjoyed our free time very much.

In March of 1943, we were restricted to the base and then taken to a railroad siding where we boarded a train. All of our movements were secret at the time. As a result, all of the curtains on the train were pulled down. We were taken to Camp Shanks in New York where we spent a short time. Our orders were to have us sent to Casablanca, but these were changed as General Eisenhower needed troops more than hospital personnel. Our new orders sent us to Fort Devens, Massachusetts, where we marched, trained and went through the infiltration courses. We crawled on our bellies while live ammunition was fired over our heads. Believe me, we learned to keep our heads down!

We were stationed at Fort Devens for a few months until orders came down sending us to England. We left for England on the 8th of October, 1943 on the luxury passenger ship Mauritania. The trip took 10 days as we zigged and zagged to avoid being torpedoed by the Nazi U-Boats, an ever-present danger in the Atlantic Ocean at the time. The ship was filled with hospital personnel, including about 150 doctors, 100 nurses and 500 enlisted hospital workers.

Most of the personnel were from Chicago. On the trip, I and many others discovered that we were not very good sailors --I was seasick for several days.

When we arrived in England, we traveled to Sudbury,

which is located in the Midlands. Our hospital was comprised of converted sheep barns serving as different wards, while we lived in Neisson Huts--six to a hut, with a pot-bellied stove in the center. We ate powdered milk and powdered eggs, although once in a while we would get a fresh egg per hut. Usually, one of the nurses would make a big pot of coffee and would add the fresh egg to the brew.

As I mentioned, the hospital had a number of different wards for medical, surgical, etc. We had some very sick patients that were in such poor condition that they were quickly sent back to the United States for treatment. For example, one of the soldiers on my ward was suffering from a brain tumor. I remember that he sent me a postcard after he left, with a picture of a beautiful rose on it. On the card was a note that said, "I wish this [rose] was real." The soldiers were so appreciative of everything we did for them and it made us feel good about being there to care for them.

One evening, when I was on duty, I accidentally bumped my knee on the corner of a bench so severely that I dislocated my patella. It was a very painful injury. My colleagues put me on one of the beds while they adjusted my patella back into place. A few days later a soldier on the bed where they had treated my dislocated patella said to me, "Lieutenant Volker, I smelled your perfume on my bed, and I could hardly sleep all night!" I got quite a laugh out of that.

On one occasion, several of us were invited to visit the local vicar and his wife for tea. The vicar's wife was an American, so we took her some Planter's Peanuts that we had gotten from the PX, as a gift. I'll never forget how she was absolutely thrilled that we brought them to her.

Once in awhile, we were able to go into London for a weekend of rest and relaxation. My friend (and fellow nurse) Una Mae English and I stayed at the Grosvenor House on one of these visits. There were anti-aircraft gun emplacements located nearby to the Grosvenor House, and I remember that they were shooting while we were there and all the windows would shake violently. It was frightening! Thank goodness there were no buzz-bombs at that time. Later, we went out for dinner with two American officers and while we were having dinner together there was an air raid. We didn't know where to go for safety and so we just stayed there in the restaurant. Meanwhile, the members of the band jumped up and ran out of the building.

Another time, we went to a play called "Lifeboat," which featured the famous actress Tallulah Bankhead. The entire performance had a scene of the ocean set in the background which looked remarkably like real water. It was so realistic, with a lifeboat swaying back and forth, that I began to feel seasick while watching the play. During the performance, the air raid light came on, but the performance continued and we stayed in the theater.

Another memory of my time in England was of an invitation to a dance by one of the Air Force doctors who was from Hutchinson, Kansas, my home state. He and his colleagues invited several of the nurses and me to a dance at their officers club. During the evening's festivities, we heard that a group of downed American pilots from our base had been rescued by the French Underground and had just been returned to our base in England. We never heard all of the details of their rescue, but we found ourselves caught up in a celebration of their return. We were so happy for them.

After we were in England for about a year, the Army brought in another general hospital unit to take our place as our unit was reassigned to Lllandudno, Wales. We were there for only a short time and I remember that we were billeted in private homes. From there, we were sent to a marshalling area back in England not long before D-Day. I remember that we all watched as many, many airplanes flew overhead on D-day. The sky was filled with airplanes.

In August 1944, we left England for France from the port at South Hampton. We crossed the channel to Cherbourg (Omaha Beach) and were taken ashore on LST boats. We were dressed in fatigues and helmets (I felt sorry for the poor GIs, who had to lug our bed rolls and supplies). To our surprise, we were happy to discover that there was an Army PX in Cherbourg where we could get the various personal items we needed. Our unit's fIrst priority when we arrived in France was to set up the tent hospital, but the front was moving so rapidly that we continued on ... rapidly to LeMans and then on to Paris where we were stationed at the Hospital Beaujon in Cliche. There were German snipers still active in Paris when we arrived. Once, when we were traveling in a convoy with our hospital personnel we heard an air raid alert. It was a scary moment as we were so exposed, but luckily no enemy aircraft ever materialized.

When our convoy first entered Paris, we could see that the Parisian people were very hungry. Several people ran up behind our ambulance hoping to get food from us as we passed through. Since we were in a convoy we had to keep going, regardless. The Germans had occupied the hospitals in Paris and prior to the liberation they had removed all of the French X-ray equipment and replaced it with their own. Ironically, the German equipment was far superior to the French and even to the best most up-to-date equipment from the United States.

Two other nurses and I had night duty on the first night of our arrival and I remember that we had to go through the entire hospital and pull down the black-out curtains. We only had three patients that first night, one of which was a soldier that had been shot in the head by a sniper. Sadly, he died later that night. I was in charge of the Medical Ward and soon we began to receive patients of all sorts. Because it was such a tense time, many of my patients suffered from conditions brought on by agitation, such as ulcers and diarrhea. Many soldiers had to be treated for "trench foot" which caused them to walk with great difficulty.

The badly wounded soldiers were sent to the field hospital first, since they were closer to the front. After they were treated at the field hospitals, they were sent back to us at the larger facilities for medical follow up and recuperation. If their injuries were extremely grave, they would be flown directly back to the States for treatment. Other than a patient who reminded me of my brother, I have few memories of specific soldiers that I nursed while I was serving in Europe. Regardless, I felt strongly that each patient in my charge was special. All of the nurses in my unit gave the very best medical care that we could and the soldiers appreciated our care so very much.

At the time, we were not aware that sugar was being rationed in the United States. I remember that when we were in Wales we contacted some of our families back home and asked them to send us Jell-O. It arrived while we were stationed in LeMans, but proved very useful after we got to Paris. Since we (both soldiers and nurses) were all eating "K" rations, powdered milk and powdered eggs, I decided to make the Jell-O for my patients and they really enjoyed the change in diet!

Although we were very busy in Paris and restricted to the hospital much of the time, I did manage to meet some interesting people along the way. We saw a performance at the famous Follies Bergeres and were able to visit a few night clubs. Of our entire stay in Paris, we were probably the most frightened during the Battle of the Bulge. I remember how the weather was so bad that our airplanes couldn't fly and we were frightened that the German army might return to occupy Paris. As you might imagine, it was a horrific time for our soldiers as well. We had so many patients in the hospital that the rooms and hallways were filled with wounded soldiers lying on gurneys. Two of my cousins were among the patients in our hospital.

I was stationed in Paris until I returned to England in 1945. At the time I had bronchitis and asthma and upon my return to England, with its damp weather, my asthma became rather severe. So, I received orders to return to the United States so that treatments could be done to alleviate my condition. I arrived back in the United States at the port of Charleston, South Carolina, on March 12, 1945. I traveled back on a hospital ship along with a colonel from Nebraska who had been shot in the knee. The Army told us we were to be sent to a hospital near to our homes, so of course we were both sent to Great Falls, Montana! After my recovery, I was given leave to return home and when my leave was over I was sent to Hot Springs, Arkansas, for some rest and recreation before my next assignment.

I had been overseas for a year and a half. Now, I was assigned to an Army hospital in Santa Barbara, California, where I worked in the obstetrics ward. It was very strange, partly because of the huge difference from my nursing duties while in the military and partly because it was the kind of work I had not done since the days of my nurse's training! The war ended and my tour of duty ended when I was mustered out from Camp Carson, Colorado on January 31, 1946.

I was asked what I hope to pass on to my grandchildren from my experience as a nurse in World War II. My feelings of "love of country" are certainly a big part of it. The realization of how wonderful life is in our country with the freedom and quality of life we have. But, even more, I loved nursing. My life has been one of service, you know, as a nurse. That's the biggest thing.

For this, my service in the military was a very worth-while experience for me. Just to watch those brave men, our soldiers, some of whom had to return to France and to the fighting --I was glad I was in a position to help. I get a great deal of pleasure and satisfaction out of doing things for other people. It makes me happy too! Caring for others helps you as much as the people you are caring for!

****

I have been widowed for 31 years. One time I ran into a wonderful friend from wartime England who was living in Minnesota, while I was living in Kansas. With the children all grown, I decided to go up north to visit her. In my fur coat and open toed shoes I felt I was making a good Midwest mix as I arrived in Minnesota. What I hadn't really planned on was liking it so well I would spend the rest of my life there. And I have!

Chapter Five

WOULD BETHESDA HAVE BEEN BETTER?

Betty Gaffney Singer, WAVE

I enlisted in the USNWR (US Navy Women's Reserve) in May 1944. After Hunter College boot camp where a friend and I accumulated 35 demerits for laughing or talking at the wrong time. I was sent to NAS Atlanta, Georgia to learn to be an air traffic tower operator. There were no books for our classes, as I believe we were only the 4th group to go through this training. We learned by taking and memorizing notes from the day-long lectures. A sailor and another WAVE from the class before, taught us.

Since I had a year of nurse's training when I enlisted, I had named Bethesda, Maryland, with its military medical care facilities, on my "dream sheet," not knowing the Navy was looking for women with deep voices. It was later I was called a "whiskey tenor" by one of the pilots in Squadron 15A.

After training, it was proudly on to NAS Kingsville, Texas, with a CAA/FCC license to work in the control tower. We all thought it was a really fun job. After all, who knows stress at 21 years old? There were two fields, North and South, where I usually worked one of three shifts, 8 a.m. to 4 p.m., 4-midnight, midnight-8 a.m.

However one time was an exception which revealed that not everyone in the Navy was used to having women aboard. One morning I had the early shift and needed to open the tower. As I walked across the field a young sailor came out of the guard shack and said, "Halt! And be recognized!" Having never heard that before, I kept on walking. But he was very, very serious and said, "My orders are no women on the field until 8 a.m." I explained that I needed to open the tower, but he was adamant. I finally talked him into calling the squadron Duty Officer, who allowed me in. I felt like Radar when he says "you dumb little kid," but refrained.

The pilot of an Army plane had spent the night, and was now readying for take-off. He needed the entire runway to get off. The Navy used only half for take-off and half for landing. So I told the Navy planes they were NOT cleared. But one got airborne, right in the propwash of the Army. I told him to return but he rocked his wings and went right on. I called the hangar to ask who was flying that plane and was told it was Ensign Stiers. To make a short story of it, that pilot came up to the tower where he learned that what we said was what was to be done! So he told me I couldn't fly a kite.

He's the man I married in August 1945.

When I had arrived at Kingsville there were 43 WAVES and about 5000 men. Most of the ladies were specialists. Our specialty patch was a diamond with a Y in the center. Much chagrin, people usually thought that meant yeoman.

I had been given only travel time to the billet, since we could have no leaves during the War emergency. We WAVES lived in tar paper-covered barracks. Discipline was pretty loose, obviously, as one gal had brought her roller skates along. And we had a piano until a WAVE officer came aboard to straighten things out.

Once I had to go to Captain's Mast. The sailor on the quarterdeck asked to see my dog tags. I said, "I don't wear those." I thought he would have a stroke. "My Lord, she comes to Mast without dog tags?" The Mast went no place when I explained the whole sequence which went something like this: I had stepped out of a car with my hat in my hand instead of on my head, making me blatantly out of uniform, in front of a woman officer who turned me in. And on another occasion I was involved in unrelated (to this time) activity which didn't help my case either. I had taken off my jacket on a hot Texas evening at a formal dance, and even worse, had advised a new-comer WAVE she could do the same.

During my time at Kingsville I learned about openings in Officer Candidate School. The thought crossed my mind that I should apply. But we were having such a good time there. No, I didn't act on the chance even though one of my superiors urged me to go for it. I wonder if Bethesda would have been that much fun.

As I said, I married the disobedient pilot. We had four sons. Two have become Vietnam veterans--one is a 22-year veteran of the Marine Corps. In 1965, Chuck was hired by NAVRSO (Navy Retail Stores Overseas) and we were sent to NAS Sangley Pt. in the Philippine Islands. In 1970 we were sent to the Panama Canal Zone for 5 years. Both tours were quite enjoyable. Sadly, Chuck had to have open heart surgery and passed away in 1985. I remarried, this time to a high school sweetheart and we had 2 good years together before he passed away also. My life is still full with following all the moves of my sons who seem to consider the whole world to be just a few stops along their way.

Chapter Six

LIFE ABOARD THE USS 'NEVERSAIL'

Marcine Nuttbrock Richmond, SPAR

How would a 20-year-old girl who grew up in a very small town in rural Oregon find herself in SPAR boot camp in Sheepshead Bay, Brooklyn, New York?

Working as a bookkeeper for The Farmers' Coop Creamery in McMinnville, she often saw this large truck with the picture of Uncle Sam on the side pointing his finger and saying, "The Navy Needs You." Feeling restless about the war and missing her Army boyfriend, she decided that perhaps the Navy would enlist her. The application was filed, but the Navy doctor rejected her based on an osteomyelitis infection when she was a young child.

This was very disappointing, and she related her story to everyone who would listen.

One listener was the bookkeeping machine repairman from Portland. His response was to try the Coast Guard. He had a female relative who had joined the SPARs and loved it. So off she went to Portland with fear and trembling and especially when encountering the question, "Have you ever been refused by another branch of the service?" After pondering this question, she marked "yes" realizing that if she marked "no" they would discover the lie and reject her for sure.

The recruiter asked the reason for the rejection and told her to let their doctor decide. Next came the physical and many questions, and to her relief and delight the doctor decided it was a risk the Coast Guard could handle. Since she was not yet 21, her parents' consent was required. Reluctantly, they signed. Her older brother was already serving with the Army Corps of Engineers in the Pacific and her younger brother was serving on a Navy troop ship back and forth across the Pacific.

In 1945 it was news that this small town girl had joined the SPARs and her picture and accompanying article appeared in the Portland *Oregonian* newspaper.

Soon she was on a train with several other recruits from Oregon headed for Sheepshead Bay, Brooklyn, NY, wherever that could be, to a boot camp named "The USS Neversail." Boot camp was strenuous but nothing like what the men endured. Even the marching was fun. Being short, she was in the last row along with the other shorties. One of those shorties lives in California and 59 years later they still keep in touch.

Only a fence separated the men and women recruits, and there were common areas among which was the long row of telephone booths. The memory has never dimmed of the 17- or 18-year-old "boy booties" as we named them, crying and talking with their families before shipping out to the War.

After completing boot camp, she went to storekeeper school in the same venue. Can you imagine an instructor in typing class trying to teach this young lady to use her right thumb instead of her left to hit the space bar after several years of typing experience? He finally relented. Thank Goodness!

Besides the work, the military had fun times going to the Roosevelt Hotel in NYC for music, teas, and dancing. They visited the Statue of Liberty, climbing to the top in the head; and went to the top of the Empire State Building, all of which was very exciting for the small town girl. There was a trip to Washington, D.C., and there were numerous trips to the beaches, but beware of getting so sunburned that you could not report for class. That was not acceptable.

At the top of the Empire State Building it's better not to look down!

Then came VJ Day in August 1945. Excitement was running high. The radio was blaring about celebrations in Times Square, and the SPARs did not want to be left out of that. After many requests they were released to go to the crowded Square in the City. But in their excitement they had almost missed seeing one SPAR sitting alone, crying.

Her husband was not coming back home. They paused to comfort her and to invite her to join them, but she declined.

Off they went to board a very crowded subway. Everyone was excited, talking and greeting each other. Finally they arrived in Times Square to find standing room only, music, lights and loudspeakers blaring the news. There was no intentional turning right or left and no number of police could direct or control the crowd. Military were everywhere. Happily, they encountered about four Coast Guard fellows who volunteered to stick with them. They were excited to learn that one of the fellows was from Oregon.

There was no room to dance and nothing programmed, so after a couple of hours of being pushed about, they managed to find their way back to the subway station. It was an experience never to be forgotten, nor was the gratitude to those Coasties who kept them safe!

Upon completion of storekeeper school, she and 13 other SPARs were sent by train to San Francisco to work in the Separation Center. They were assigned to a separate car and to their amazement there appeared a lieutenant in the Air Force with them who perhaps is still wondering how he got into that car with all those women! That trip took many days as time was spent on sidings to allow more important War-related cargo to pass.

In San Francisco, the SPARs were barracksed in a residential hotel on Sutter Street where the Shore Patrol protected them and taught them to shoot pool. The Separation Center was located in the Simmons Mattress Company warehouse on Fisherman's Wharf. The logical transportation was the cable car which added to their daily fun. When the points required for separation were lowered, there were many more men who passed through the Center and that required long hours of work. A few resented the rates the SPARs held since it appeared to them to be unfair. However, most of the men were so grateful to be on their way out and receiving their final pay, that they could not care less.

It was a sad day when it was announced that the center was closing and all of the reserve Coast Guard would be discharged and sent home. They computed their own final pay and typed out the discharges. Special friendships have spanned the years.

Her career in accounting continued and she retired from Soil Conservation Service, part of the Department of Agriculture with 30 years of service. At one of the retiree functions, she met the daughter of another retiree and discovered they had the same unusual first name, Marcine.

The lady told this story. She was born in 1945. Her parents had brought her home from the hospital without naming her and soon someone from the hospital called asking for her name for the records. She said that her father told her that he was reading the paper, saw an article and spotted the name Marcine. Both ladies agree that he must have seen the picture and article that was in the paper when she enlisted in the SPARs. What a coincidence that was to bring those ladies together to become good friends!

The Oregon SPARs are fortunate to have a very active leader who plans or recruits planners for annual reunions. They meet at Coast Guard stations along the coast and are graciously hosted by Coast Guard personnel. Since SPARs are an "endangered species," there are fewer every year who are able to attend.

Her year in the SPARs was a valuable experience, which broadened her horizons and created opportunities to see more of the United States and to meet many people. Schools in her district invite military and former military to speak to and interact with the students on every Veterans Day. She wears her SPAR slacks, shirt, jacket and hat, to the surprise of many including herself. She will always be a SPAR.

****

I have been married to William Richmond for 45 years. He brought two boys to our marriage, Dick age 12 ½ years and Joe, 10 years old. They joined my two children, Terry age 8, and Renee, age 7. We have many rich memories of our life so far in the same house for 45 years.

Chapter Seven

I WOKE UP THE ARMY!
(The US Army's First Female Bugler)
Donna-Mae Smith, WAAC

I was born January 3, 1920 in a small railroad town called Manly in Iowa. My father was an engineer on the Rock Island Railroad and my mother was a housewife. I was one of three girls. Through the years, as Dad had more seniority, we moved from Iowa to Minneapolis/St Paul area where we attended various schools.

For awhile we were located in St. Paul Park, Minnesota, a suburb of St. Paul where my sisters and I all graduated from high school. To attend schools of higher learning we had to travel to St. Paul and Minneapolis where I attended Minneapolis School of Music and had a brief stint at U of M.

In grade and high school in St. Paul Park we were enrolled in a band directed by L.L. Wittbecker who had at one time been a member of John Phillip Sousa's band. I played trumpet in the school band, and my sister played clarinet. While attending high school I was enrolled in Brown and Bigelow Adv. Co. Drum and Bugle Corps and in 3M Company Band; also in Dyer Bros. Music Co. Band. We played and marched in St. Paul's Winter Carnival parades and in Minneapolis Aquatennial parades during the summer. We also played in the Payne Avenue Drum and Bugle Corps Unit. My sister was the drum major and I was a bugler. We had lots of fun.

After graduating high school I still took private trumpet lessons from Mr. Wittbecker and went to work for West Publishing Co., a law book publishing company, as a proof-reader. In the evenings I would travel from St. Paul to U of M or Minneapolis College of Music for the courses I took there, and late at night I would take the last bus home to sleep. On Saturdays I would go to St. Paul again to play in the band that Dyer brothers had each Saturday morning.

In June and July of 1942 an ad ran in the St. Paul Pioneer Press and Dispatch newspaper about the government needing women musicians to join an all-women band in a group known as the WAAC - Womens Army Auxiliary Corps. I responded and within a matter of a very few days received a letter stating I was to report for duty at once. Shortly after, I received two telegrams in one day stating it was "imperative" I respond. I had my physical in Minneapolis and was on my way to Ft. Des Moines, Iowa. I cried all the way, never having been away from my folks or home. I was 22 years old and very inexperienced in traveling other than to visit my grandmother in Mason City, Iowa.

So there we were at the station in Des Moines, Iowa,

and were met by GI trucks into which we were expected to climb aboard and sit on benches. The post was at least 15 miles away and we were all scared to death. This was August 13, 1942.

Fort Des Moines had been a cavalry post in prior years. The building out of which our clothing was issued had recently been used as horse stables and you could still smell the odors. Fortunately the band was housed in Officer Quarter buildings right across the street from the PX. So our housing was really great if you can appreciate double deck bunks in a room holding about 30 beds. Also, don't forget the shots we all lined up to receive.

Our day room was large, so was used as a day room in the evenings but a practice room for the entire band during the day. We set up chairs and music stands for 35-50 people. We used closets as lockers and solo practice rooms, and any other available space we could find. One room was used as an office and one small room was used for the 1st sergeant. In the basement were the latrines and showers, laundry and ironing room. Upstairs on 2nd floor more large rooms were used for many cots and bunks. All clothing issued was khaki color--what a sight that was--except for our girdles and garter belts. Yes, we wore girdles and/or garter belts to keep our GI issue cotton stockings up. No more silk or nylon hose. There was a war on! In my case, the Army didn't realize that women could be tall and large, so my 5'11" height and my size 12 shoes became a logistic problem. They had to order my shoes for me and I was forced to wear my civilian brown shoes which did not fit with cotton stockings in them! I had foot problems from the beginning and visited sick bay often, being told by many new officers that I was "out of uniform" until word finally got around that Supply was unable to supply some WAACs with proper clothing. It was about 8 weeks before I was finally "shod."

The purpose of the band was to recruit women for the WAAC and to train band members for other posts that were being newly opened in other states. We had a nucleus of 40 or 50 members and as our ranks swelled to 75 or 80 we would release 30 or so members to send to another post.

Some members were sent to Warrant Officer School and that was probably the first mistake I made in the service, not taking the opportunity to go when it was offered to me. However, I was solo 1st chair trumpet and as such was asked to play bugle calls for the Post. That's the way I became the 1st Woman Bugler in the US Army. A writeup in the newspaper stated, "Mpls WAAC Gets Privilege of Rousing Post."

For recruiting we traveled to Lincoln, Nebraska; Peoria, Illinois; Chicago, Minneapolis, St. Paul and other nearby states. We were welcomed heartily wherever we traveled to play. We were exempt from calisthenics and KP, as we got plenty of exercise playing for the Friday parades on the Post.

Mrs. Eleanor Roosevelt and Olveta Culp Hobby, the Director of the WAAC, visited our Post and I was able to shake hands with them and take a snapshot of them together. I still have it in my scrapbook. Every Friday we fell out for a parade on the grounds and all the dignitaries of the Post attended. How great we all marched and WOW, we all looked so great--such precision!

During this time I met several of the men stationed at Fort Des Moines, especially the fellows of the MP, for it was out of that office that I reported for bugle duty. But I'm getting ahead of myself. Each morning the Officer of the Day would call my barracks to notify me it was time to arise and get ready, and be at the Post cannon, which was in front of the Provost Marshall's office, to play 1st Call and Reveille. Stationed there were the MPs who guarded the Post and any prisoners that were incarcerated there. During the ensuing months I was able to meet not only the MPs, but also the male band members who were shipping overseas when we WAACs replaced them.

I had two suitors. One was named Walt and the other was Bob. Neither was aware that I was dating both of them at the same time. Walt would take me to a movie early in the evening and bring me home early as he had to rise early, and Bob would pick me up after. We would play cards in the day room or go for a late walk. Walt shipped out to go to cook school and while he was gone, Bob proposed to me and I accepted! We were married in the Chaplain's home on the Post on January 29, 1943 with many band members and MPs present.

Irving Berlin wrote *"Someday I'm going to murder the bugler, Someday they're going to find him dead, And then I'll get the other pup, the guy that gets the bugler up, And spend the rest of my life in bed."* Well, by now you have to know I married the guy that got the bugler up!

We received permission to live off Post. Our first place was one room which we rented in an elderly lady's home, within walking distance to the Post, and with an outhouse out the back path! Our next was a 3-room house, kitchen, bedroom and living room. It was fun decorating it.

In the meantime, recruiting had gone so well they had to expand Ft. Des Moines to accommodate an additional 5,000 women. They called this area Boomtown. In July of 1943 the WAAC was such a tremendous success the government decided to drop the auxiliary part of WAAC and make it Womens Army Corps, WAC, and as such, they requested that we sign a new contract. Because I was pregnant, I opted not to rejoin. I was discharged in August 1943 and lived off Post until baby Craig was born at Ft. Des Moines Hospital on the base. Bob had been shipped out about two weeks earlier to a camp in Galesburg, Illinois. So after Craig was born I went home to my parents and lived there for about three months before joining my husband in Illinois. Bob was then shipped to Camp White, Oregon, out of Medford, Oregon, and I traveled there to be with him.

In 1947 I was contacted by Jay Hormel of the Hormel Packing Co. I was asked if I would come to Austin, Minnesota to meet at his home regarding joining a new American Legion Post he was forming to take back to New York City for the American Legion parade there. He was forming a post for all women veterans and wished to form a Drum and Bugle corps to march in the parade. I was to be the house mother to 65 girls. We would train at the Stamford Academy in Stamford, Connecticut, for 1 month before being taken to the parade in NYC to compete. I agreed to go and be the leader of the parade. We had a fabulous time training and marching at the academy grounds even though we did raise a few objections from the neighbors within hearing distance. We marched in the parade and won, I believe, a 2nd prize. A month or so after I returned home, Jay Hormel called me again with a proposal that I be hired by the Hormel Co. to be house mother to the same group of lady veterans to be in his sales crew traveling from city to city demonstrating Hormel Products. I told him I was married and that I also had a small baby. Craig was only two at the time. He said, "No problem, bring him along and we'll hire a nanny to watch him during the day." So we all went. We each made $50 a week with all expenses paid. That included hair salon once a week, all meals and hotels. Jay was a very generous man. And for all this, each team of 4 girls had its own car to drive to neighborhoods to advertise and go door to door handing out our cards and coupons for Hormel Products. In the evening we ladies played as a jazz band and entertained. I stayed with the group until November 1947, then decided I no longer wanted to travel. The Hormel Co. recently contacted me and sent me a video of those days.

In 1948 our second son was born. We worked to make ends meet, moving to California. In 1955 our youngest son was diagnosed with leukemia and died within the week. Bob and I were both devastated. Nine years later Bob died of carcinoma of the lungs. I remarried a year later to a man named Ed. We moved to Nevada and stayed there 18 years before moving to Oregon. In 1996 Ed passed away with a heart attack.

I currently serve as Commander of the American Legion Post 152 in Oakland, Oregon, having held that post for 4 years. I also belong to the American Women Veterans Association in Roseburg and to the Amvets in the same town.

****

I now look back on my career in the military with gratitude, honored that I was able to serve. I remain in the home and keep busy with my china painting and playing Taps for

Donna-Mae Smith

First Woman Bugler
United States Army
Then and now...serving her country

In 1942, Donna-Mae Baldeneicker-Bott-Smith became our nation's First Woman Bugler while serving in the United States Army. A resident of Sutherlin, Oregon, to this day, at the age of 81, she still volunteers her time and talent to bid our veteran's farewell, military style by playing taps at their funerals. For more information on Smith and other women veteran's contact or visit the Women's War Memorial, Washington, D.C.

funerals of veterans.

Last year our VFW Honor Guard served at 108 funerals for veterans. So far this year I am averaging about 3 funerals a week. I deem it a great privilege to comfort veterans' families in their time of need and am very thankful that I can still play my trumpet at these occasions.

Chapter Eight

PENICILLIN, AUTOCLAVES & MUSTARD PLASTERS

Kathleen Godsil Sewell, Cadet Nurse Corps

$\mathbf{W}$hen I thought about writing my memories of the Cadets, I wondered if I could remember that far back. Sixty years is a long, long time; however, many memories did come flooding back. It was fun remembering and making contact with some of my old Cadet friends.

In May 1943 I graduated from high school in Deer Lodge, a small community in western Montana. The times were troubled with our country in the midst of World War II. Many of our classmates had enlisted while still in high school.

After graduation, five of our class were accepted into the Sisters of Charity School of Nursing that was affiliated with Carroll College in Helena, Montana.

Shortly after being accepted in the school, we applied for a new scholarship program signed into law by President Franklin Roosevelt to relieve the desperate need for professionally trained nurses in the military and civilian hospitals. Lucille Petry, RN, headed a very successful recruiting program under Public Health Services with advanced educational standards for diploma schools with approved hospitals. It was a most successful program and 124,000 nurses graduated before the War ended.

As members, we received a $15 monthly stipend, tuition and financial aid to complete our diploma, after which we agreed to be available for military or essential civilian service for the duration of the War. The government issued uniforms, designed by a leading designer, which consisted of a winter uniform of gray wool jacket, skirt, and overcoat with a belted back and red epaulets on the shoulders and silver insignia buttons. The hat for winter was a side dropped beret in gray felt with a silver shield of an eagle, anchor and caduceus. Black pump shoes completed the ensemble. The summer uniform was in the same style, but made of chambray. It was not compulsory to wear the uniforms except for such special occasions as parades. However, we found we did get special attention if we did wear them!

It was quite a shock to be free from school in May and back to loads of books and classes in June. It took some adjusting to go from living in a quiet home to living in a bustling dorm at Immaculate Hall and about 100 gals.

Parents packed us up and drove us the 60 miles over the Continental Divide to our new life. We all had young dreams of topping Florence Nightingale and saving the world. We did not have any drill sergeants, but the nuns provided a bit of discipline. My cousin Mary B. from Butte and several of her friends were in the class and living at the dorm with us. To expedite the number of nurses needed for the War, we had four months of intensive pre-clinical class work at Carroll College, followed by training at one of three Montana hospitals: St. James in Butte, St. Vincent in Billings, and our home hospital, St. John's in Helena. After four months, we had a capping ceremony and went to our chosen hospitals where classes and practical duty in the hospital continued under strict supervision.

Carroll College was a private boy's school prior to WWII. After the war started, the Navy, (V12 and V5) took over some of the college, mostly premedical and pre-dental students, so unlike most colleges there was no shortage of dates for Cadet nurses. We were much in demand!

Immaculate Hall was a nice three-story brick building with classrooms, library, offices, laundry, and a kitchen where we gathered for popcorn, candy and chats in the evening. The second floor auditorium was great for dances, plays and classes. There was a formal "parlor" in French Provincial style, with large fireplace, where our dates waited in full view of our petite housemother. Curfew was at 9 p.m. week evenings and bed check, with everyone in bed with lights out, was 10 p.m. Ha! We did have a structured existence with lots of classes and study time, but we had fun, too.

Weekdays we were up by 6 a.m. and earlier if we decided to go to mass at the hospital chapel. To sleep longer, we rolled our PJ's up and threw a coat over them and raced across the street to the hospital, still trying to stifle our giggles when someone's PJ's fell down at chapel. We did some praying while sitting there wondering what time the nuns had to get up to look so perfect in their habits. Breakfast was at seven, and then we had classes all day and studied in the evening. Sometimes we walked down the hill to the Parrot Confectionary for a coke or one of their famous hot fudge sundaes with the hot fudge served in separate little pitchers. We also went window shopping at the elegant Flegelman's Dept. Store. We were free on weekends during our pre-clinic, and the Deer Lodge group usually headed home on a bus until Sunday evening. One weekend we invited a few of the V12's to go with us to Rock Creek Lake outside of Deer Lodge where two of the Cadet parents had cabins.

Our mothers did the cooking and chaperoning and it

Jiny, Rita, Jen, Bets, Kay

was a special occasion for all of us. Bless them, they were happy to put us all on the bus back to college.

During our pre-clinic time, we helped three of our Deer Lodge gals, Betty B., Connie E., and Stella H., to elope with their high school loves. That left Betty M. and me to graduate, and we remained roommates until we finished. By then we had many really good friends. Lola Mae from Wolf Creek, Montana,was one of us and we three have remained special friends.

Helena, where Carroll College is located, is an old gold mining town in the mountains and is the Montana capital. The old wealth was evident in elegant three and four story brick mansions, most of which had survived a devastating earthquake in 1935. The old St. John's Hospital was still standing like a ghost on the campus, but had been condemned. For some reason, we never ventured inside. I guess we followed the rules, but we often found ingenious ways to get around them, which was most of the fun.

After our pre-clinical time, all of us received our much-coveted caps in a Capping Ceremony and got on with actual patient care. We went to our chosen hospitals where classes and practical duty continued under strict supervision. Off we went with well-starched uniforms and caps (no black band on our caps until after graduation), white hose and ugly, sensible white shoes, which were really a blessing for the many miles we walked for three years. We often worked split shifts (7-4, 3-11, or 11-7). Our only time off was one day a week and a summer vacation of one week. At first, what we lacked in experience we made up for with youthful enthusiasm.

Because we lived in an earthquake area, part of our training included earthquake drill, especially being responsible for our charges, the patients, but all we had were a few tremors.

Our first patient was a wonderful old bachelor who had been living alone without proper nutrition and care, had worn bedsores and had developed a huge decubitus. It was an unexpected initiation for us! However, he received the best care in the world and after a few months, we sent our favorite patient home with help. This, however, did not match the unrealistic Cadet Nurse recruiting posters. I still marvel at what we accomplished with care and lots of love.

Another patient was a delightful, very old Monsignor from Belgium. He had been a brilliant man but was quite senile. We tried to keep him happy and we young nurses quickly discovered if we sat him outside on the second floor porch with rails around it, he thought he was on a ship going across the ocean. Now I wish I had a picture of him in his glory, all decked out in his clerical robes!

Bets reminded me of the day when it was quiet on the medical floor, and we filled a syringe with a horrible tasting cough syrup and injected it into the center of some luscious chocolate candy in a box. We left it on the desk, knowing how the doctors loved candy. Their faces were wonderful as they headed for the nearest wastebasket, but I'm sure they got even with us. They were very good teachers and rarely lost patience with us.

One night after a formal dance at the college, we came back to our dorm and learned that one of our nurses from Deer Lodge was about to go into surgery for an emergency appendectomy. Still dressed for the dance, we dashed to the hospital to be with Lois, and I remember the doctor looking at us and saying, "Had I known this was formal, I'd have worn my spats." Lois recovered well, but we were grounded for coming in late.

One of our Deer Lodge friends, Lolly B., spent her Cadet Nurse Corps in Baltimore at Johns Hopkins. They had such advantages as having Eleanor Roosevelt and Helen Keller as speakers, but she said the Corps was much the same there. It was a 1000 bed hospital and covered four city blocks. The nursing home (Hampton Hours) was seven stories and connected to the hospital by an underground tunnel. They could sneak out that way at night, but we had to use the first floor windows. The head of the Cadet Corps, Lucille Petry, was a graduate of Johns Hopkins Hospital.

We all rotated and were assigned different areas for a period of time: medicine, surgery, obstetrics, pediatrics, nursery, public health, diet kitchen, lab, emergency room, communicable diseases at the state TB hospital in Galen, and psychiatry at the state hospital in Warm Springs. The last six months of our training, we were usually assigned head nurse positions in one of the departments. Because of nursing shortages, I chose the pediatric ward. It was before vaccines were developed for polio, diphtheria and whooping cough. Sometimes patients with polio, which caused paralysis and sometimes death, were sent to hospitals equipped with iron lungs. These were metal ventilators where patients with collapsed respiratory systems were placed, sometimes indefinitely. The sound these machines made was very eerie.

It seemed as if everyone had their children's tonsils removed, which was standard practice at that time. Parents were permitted only limited visits at that time because the administration thought the children were difficult to handle when the parents were around. I am glad things have changed.

One of our pediatric patients was Charlie, a hydrocephalic baby whose head kept growing because of excessive accumulation of cerebral fluid within the cranium, for which there was no medical remedy at the time. He was the sweetest baby with a face like an angel that is still clear in my memory. We all adored Charlie and really cried when he left us. Now there are ventricular shunts that would have helped him, but he was born a few years too soon.

I remember when we gave the first injection of penicillin after it was discovered. What a breakthrough it was for our troops, the Home Front, and the world. I think the most potent drug we had before that was sulfa. They even had a picture in the newspaper of six of my classmates, which was captioned, "Giving a Penicillin Shot." I sent the clipping to my sister with a note assuring her that it really took only one nurse to give the shot. Once an older doctor ordered a mustard plaster for one of his patients. This was an old time remedy for chest colds and pneumonia, and we really had to scramble to find a recipe for a mustard plaster.

It could be left on the chest only a short time because it could burn the skin easily. We were up to the challenge . That was the last time I ever saw one, thank heaven.

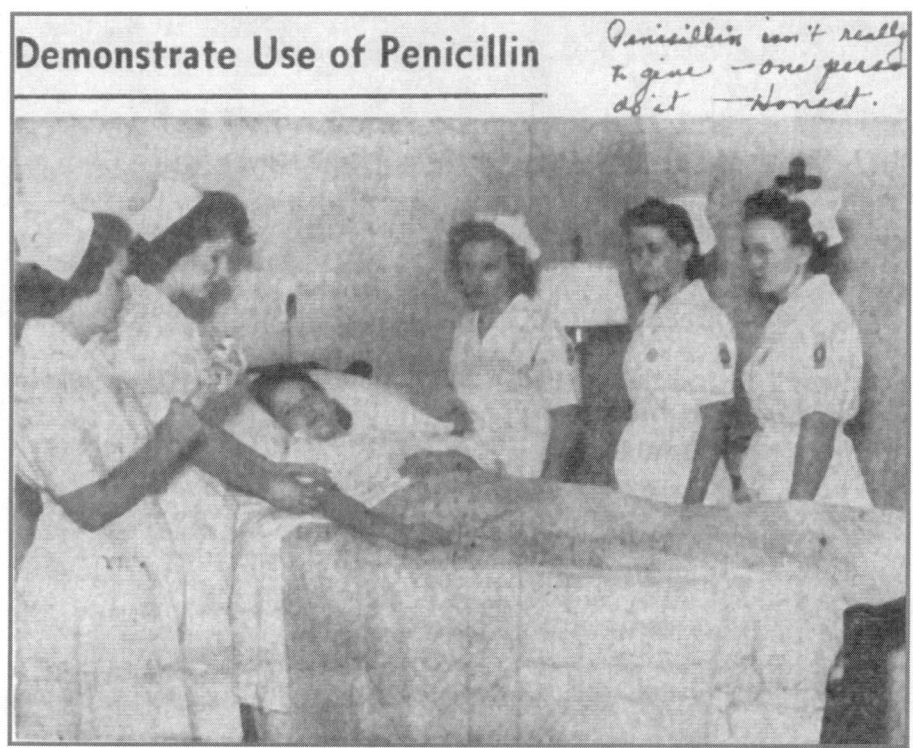

Demonstrate Use of Penicillin

Penicillin isn't really to give —one per of it —Honest.

To say that we were not a throwaway society would be an understatement. We boiled and autoclaved everything. Each med room had a small boiler, and we boiled glass syringes and needles for reuse. We even sharpened needles. We wrapped various packs after cleaning for autoclaving and reuse. We moved heavy oxygen tanks on dollies and were expert at changing the gauges, cracking the tanks, and never dropping one of these monsters.

One day while on surgery duty, I decided the surgery straps should be sterilized and I autoclaved them. If you have never seen what happens to leather when autoclaved, just contact me. Surprisingly, everyone quite understood and maybe even laughed about it later.

Not a day went by that we did not worry and pray for our relatives and friends who were in the actual battle, especially my boyfriend at the time who was a captain flying B17's over Germany in the 8th Air Force. We did not know or would not have believed the extent of the evil Hitler was

Reading left to right: Row 1- Jinx Jennings, Dude Watkins, Jo McGowan, Kay Godsil, Kay Berberet, Ann Miroslavich   Row 2 - Betty Gunderson, Gen Morresette, Deanna Peterson, Rita Mae Lanning, Eileen D'Arcy   Row 3 - Betty Myrah, Lola Davis, Ruth Woods, Anne Robbins

doing. We all had dreams of what we would do after graduation. Mine was to be a flight nurse, but the war ended before we graduated, so we went our separate ways with many opportunities open to us due to our very good education.

By the Act of Congress, I do believe nursing education was advanced and standardized so that many RN's have been able to get a BS, MS, and PhD in nursing. When we sang the Cadet Nurse song, *"We're Cadets, we're in the Corps, doing our part to help a nation win a war,"* we did not realize that we actually did staff the hospitals, freeing many nurses to go in the services. The Cadet Nurse Corps was not only a great benefit to the War effort, but also to the future of nursing.

****

After graduation I worked at St. Barnabas Hospital in Minneapolis, Minnesota, and was later accepted as a stewardess for Northwest Airlines. Loved the flying, and still do. I stayed about 6 years, then married a Deer Lodge classmate, Jack Sewell, who had been in school at the University of Minnesota. We lived in Denver, Colorado, before returning to Montana. Our family grew to 4: Mark, Joan, Aileen and Paul. I now have many grandchildren and 3 "greats." Wow! Unfortunately,Jack died suddenly in 1976, but that wonderful man is still with us in memory. Once again my RN served me well and back to work I went until I retired at 69. Retirement is great!

Chapter Nine

FOUR FROM ONE FAMILY

Mary Libes Weatherman, WAVE

Being a WWII Navy WAVE was a proud thing for me. I arrived at Hunter College in August 1943 for the boot camp experience to be lived out in Bldg II, Apt 2G, Reg 11. It was my first time out of North Carolina and my first train ride. I slept on the train and pulled into New York just as I was waking up. I was all alone and scared to death ... 20 years old, from an old Southern family. I didn't know nothing from nothing! My sister Elsie, one year older, joined the WACs and the other sister, Ruby, joined the Coast Guard as a SPAR. One went to Florida and the other to California. My only brother, Allen, had joined the Air Force and was overseas.

I did not finish high school because we took jobs to help out the family. My mother had 5 children, my dear dad was a house builder, and we had no money. No one was needing houses built, so there was no work.

Mary Libes may not be a pilot, but she knows how to pose in an SNYJ

Right away I learned to love the Navy uniforms, even the seersucker one. The dress and whites were "sharp as tacks." The medical part I could have done without. The shots, how I hated them. We could not raise our arms the next day. I had never had a complete physical examination and when the doctor gave me an internal, I thought I would die!

After boot, when I got my assignment to Texas, I was surprised to find I was going to Corpus Christi Naval Air Station. One other WAVE and I were traveling together and I was in charge. We checked in at night. The next morning I looked at that HUGE base, and WOW! What am I doing here? Anyway, I went all over that base, finally finding my way to the WAVE barracks.

I wanted to take a shower but you know how that was ...I could not undress in front of strangers, so back to my bunk I went. After awhile I went back to the shower and more girls were there. Finally, I stepped out of my robe and into the shower. Oh, I was embarrassed to tears!

On my first liberty a WAVE friend, also from North Carolina, and I went to a fancy hotel and took a seat in the lobby. This big black man in a red coat came up and asked if we wanted a drink. Here I am, 20 years old and never had a drink. We had heard about a Tom Collins, so that was our order. Whew! What an awful taste.

Yes, I had grown up in the South. A black person never walked in my section of town. No school, no restaurant, no drinking fountains, and no restrooms for them. I don't know who decided that, but that's the way it was here until the 1950s.

Everywhere we walked proudly, with people staring at us, as we felt "I'm in the Navy now." There were occasional insults or comments we had to listen to about women in uniform, but we knew why we were there doing what we were doing.

After two weeks at Corpus Christi I was sent to Kingsville Air Field, a small field on the Mexican border. One hundred fifty WAVES, and 3000 cadets getting their wings! Without any special training, I was assigned to do a little bit of everything. But oh, how I wanted to be a control tower operator. We had F4Fs and SNJs. My job was wherever I was needed. The tower, the hangar or the storeroom. I had to keep count of planes. One time in the tower, while the operators were chatting and not paying attention, there was an SNJ "in the groove" who still had his gear up. I grabbed the microphone and said, "Plane in the groove, take a wave-off, your wheels are up!" Boy, the Duty Officer called the tower and wanted to know who was on duty. There were some reprimands handed out on that one. But I was really proud of myself.

Tower was just one of my many assignments. We were lucky girls as we had flight time allowed to us. That meant more money. The guys were glad to take us WAVES for a

WAVES grouped on the steps of "Personnel," waiting to begin the paperwork for separation from the service.

ride. That way they had a chance to scare us with their spins, dives and rollovers.

My first leave from Texas was a learning experience. The trains were full of service men, so full many were sitting in the aisles on duffel bags. I had a stopover in Houston and called my old Sunday School teacher. She picked me up and we had a visit, which was nice. When I made it home I was so happy to see Allen, on furlough R & R from overseas, and Elsie who also was able to come home. Ruby did not make it. Allen had landed in California just 14 miles from where Ruby was stationed but didn't know she was there, so they missed a good chance of seeing each other.

My good friend Barney was put on restriction one time because of her beautiful blonde hair which had grown too long. Regs declared that it must not touch the collar in back. She already had a date set up which would happen during that restriction time, so could not go off base. She asked me if I had plans that night. I did not, so her date, who had a big long convertible, put her in the back, put the top down and drove out the gate. I slept in her bunk for night check. Oh, we had fun.

Our barracks were called "Tar Paper Palaces" and we had a guard house to keep the men out. "The men" were 4 squadrons, two at 14 A&B and two at 15 A&B. Most of the WAVES worked at the squads and with the pilots, therefore we dated officers. The sailors called us "officer bait" because of that. I had a pilot friend of mine visit me here in North Carolina in the 1960s while he was on a business trip. We had so much fun talking about the "good old days." My husband just listened to us--he was an Air Force man.

I also had a dear friend who was a CPO over the band. He and his family lived off base. I was invited to their place quite often and it was nice to visit inside a home. Also, I met two young girls from Corpus Christi who dated pilots in Kingsville. They came to the base often to pick me up and take me home with them.

VE Day was one happy occasion. The pilots flew all around the base in all directions. No one cared as we were all so happy. We WAVES knew we would be going home soon. I was discharged in December 1945. That was a sad time for all of us because we had become good friends. Two of my dear friends were from Ohio. Both married pilots, one Navy and the other Marine. One is now in Florida, and the other has passed on.

I will always be proud of my 2 ½ years as a Navy WAVE. This past 4th of July at my church as the music was sung, tears spilled over. Don't ask why ...I don't know. It was just something about being proud, I'm sure. I am now nearly 82 years old and the war was a long time ago. But I'll never forget, not even my Service Number 745-77-33!

****

After the War I worked for Hanes Hosiery Company for 6 years. I left there when Western Electric came to Winston-Salem, retiring after 23 years. I had married at age 34, finally finding the right guy! My only child, a daughter April, is now 45 years old.

Chapter Ten

MOM & DAD STAYED HOME!

Elsie Libes Boyer, WAAC/WAC

I have two sisters who went into the service after I did. Mary Libes Weatherman went into the WAVES, and Ruby Libes Vogler joined the Coast Guard SPARs. Our father was in World War I in France, and our brother Allen was overseas as a gunner on a bomber at the same time we three sisters were serving. Mom and Dad were left home alone.

I joined the WAACs in 1942, before they became officially known as the Women's Army Corps, WAC. I was sent to Oglethorpe, Georgia for basic training. After basic I was sent to Fort Meyers, Florida, Buckingham Army Air Force Base.

There were about 5,000 pilots and gunners being trained there, and only about 100 WACs. What a place to be!

The WACs had their own barracks on the base. However, the building was not air conditioned, and was hot as a furnace in the summer.

My duty was in the Flight Surgeon's office where it was my job to help process the gunners and pilots through to the pressure chamber in the back part of the building. I checked their eyes as they went in, and their ears as they came out. This pressure chamber procedure was necessary due to the lack of sophistication of the oxygen systems for pilots and gunners who needed clear heads at high altitudes. It was necessary to learn how they would perform in the air.

As soon as I arrived in Florida I met this gal from New Jersey name Genevieve Obeleski. We hit it off right away. We still are friends to this day, and see each other as often as we can. After each of us got married, we four would get together, until my husband passed away. Genevieve and I both worked in the hospital. She worked in the lab.

We had so much fun on duty in Florida. Gene and I would go to a cabin that was kept especially for the WACs at the beach, and spend the weekend. We got into the habit of changing into civvies after leaving the base. But that came to an abrupt halt by something that happened one time. There was an MP who I'm sure didn't like us very well, maybe because we were always dating officers. He always seemed to follow us around. One time when we had gone to our hotel room, changed clothes and come back down, he was waiting in the lobby. He followed us for a bit, then arrested us and put us in jail. Our Commanding Officer had to send someone down to get us out of the pokey. The MP got shipped overseas not too long after that. Did we mind?

Usually on weekends we would go into town, meet guys, dance all evening to the juke boxes. Our lives were full of fun after duty hours.

I am very proud to have been in the Women's Army Corps.

The three Libes "girls" left to right: Ruby (SPAR) Mary (WAVE Elsie (WAC)

****

My husband, who was an Army veteran of 8 years, with time in New Caledonia, died in 1997. Together we had 2 children, and now I have 3 grandchildren and 2 great-grandchildren. I went to Washington, D.C. in 1995 for the groundbreaking of the Women's Memorial. Since its opening, I have sent part of one of my uniforms for revolving display, along with my picture. It was because of my sister Mary that I learned about this chance to tell my story about being in the WACs.

50-year friends meet to celebrate the new Military Women's Memorial in Washington, D.C., in the background

Elsie Libes Boyer is on the left, with her Army buddy "Jean" Obelinski Olterzewski alongside.

Two WAC buddies from years past find themselves guarded by the Marines at the dedication of the Women's Memorial Monument.

Familiar World War II WAVES poster. Most of the service women were sure that at the end of boot or basic they would look just like the poster girls.

Chapter Eleven

IMPORTANT THINGS LIKE SHOES, HOME COOKING & SLEEP

Vera Hendricks Hampton, WAVE

During the six weeks we spent in boot camp we marched everywhere, from the mess hall to class, to drill practice, back to barracks. Why I remember is that I had been issued shoes too small. I wore size 7½. At first the size 6 shoes did not seem too small, but after a few weeks of constant walking, it began to tell on me. In my letter home I said, "Sometimes my corns yell at each other so loud it's a wonder some officer didn't tell them to PIPE DOWN!"

In fact, one of the ditties we sang as we marched really applied to me:

The shoes that they gave us
They say are mighty fine
You asked for number sixes
They gave you number nines!

But I still love the Navy
And I don't want to go home

When friends ask why I did not complain about my feet, I can only say that we had been taught to ignore the small unimportant things, and my sore toes must have fit under the unimportant category.

We were kept busy with drill practice, classroom lectures on Naval history, and keeping our living quarters "ship-shape". There was no time for luxuries such as soaking in a warm tub filled with hot water. However, the last few days spent there were much more relaxing, and we spent time planning our futures, and had chances to play little tricks on our roommates. One such day a roommate called "Bobbie" decided to soak in a nice warm bubble bath. It was after "lights out," when everyone was supposed to be in bed. Bobbie was thoroughly enjoying herself when someone tapped on the bathroom door. Thinking it was one of her roommates, she sang out, "Who's that knocking at my door?" The door opened and there stood the 2nd Lieutenant who terminated the tub fun.

My assignment after boot was to yeoman training school at Stillwater, Oklahoma. Now we WAVES found ourselves traveling again. We went from New York City to Stillwater, Oklahoma, the scenic route. Our group of women must not have been considered top priority because they sent our train a roundabout route through northern New York state across Canada to Windsor, then Detroit, Michigan, south to Chicago and south again through Illinois, Missouri and finally Oklahoma.

Many times our cars were left sitting on a siding while

other trains passed. The summer days went slowly. The WAVE officer in charge of our group must have felt a little bored too, as she gave the order to muster on the platform near a railroad station. The order was not well received because it was a warm evening, many girls were ready for bed, some with hair in curlers. When we did gather on the station platform, we hoped the local citizens were not watching too closely. Hats had been jammed on uncombed hair, some legs were bare. No one seemed to care, and after trying to keep order walking up and down the uneven platform, we were sent back to our car. As usual, we were kept in the dark about the reason for that exercise.

WHAT PAY DOES A NAVY WAVE GET?

RATE	Monthly Base Pay–Clear	Food Allowance*	Quarters Allowance*	Total Monthly Income
Apprentice Seaman	$50.00	$54.00	$37.50	$141.50
Seaman Second Class	54.00	54.00	37.50	145.50
Seaman First Class	66.00	54.00	37.50	157.50
Petty Officers	78.00 to 126.00	54.00	37.50	169.50 to 217.50

*(Unless food and quarters are provided by Navy)

PLUS $200. for clothing, the finest medical and dental care, special tax exemption, low-cost Government life insurance, and free mail, reduced rates on transportation, theater tickets, etc.

After finishing my training at yeoman school at Stillwater, I was assigned to the Naval Supply Depot at Oakland, California. I was allowed a few days of leave before reporting to Oakland and was eagerly looking forward to some home cooked meals. We had traveled by coach on the train for three days between Oklahoma and California, and by the time I arrived in Fresno, California, I was totally exhausted. Never in my life have I been able to sleep while sitting upright. So I found myself sitting in the Fresno bus station at 0200 waiting for the Greyhound bus to take me the rest of my journey to Modesto, my home town.

When the bus driver arrived, I was sound asleep, alone in the tiny waiting room. The driver woke me and announced that my bus was waiting for me, then he disappeared. I picked up my suitcase and headed out the door. There was the bus, but I could find NO DOOR. I knew there must be one somewhere, but this bus had no door! What could I do? The driver had disappeared and the %$# bus had no door!! So I returned to the waiting room. Soon a frustrated, impatient driver appeared. This time he led me to the open door. I didn't bother to try to explain to the poor guy. He probably would not have believed me anyway. The rest of the journey was a blur in my mind. I did enjoy my leave at home, then went on to Oakland for the rest of the War.

In Oakland I was assigned as yeoman to the Naval Supply Depot, which sat right next to the Alameda Naval Air Station. Both were on the east side of the Bay. I was assigned to the Provisions and Ships Store Stock branch of the depot.

The Navy had no place to house us right away, as out barracks had not been built. So we were housed in boarding houses out in East Oakland. It cost the Navy $60 per month to house us. On payday our landlady was sitting in the lobby when we got home. I shared my room with two other WAVES on the 2nd floor, with one bathroom for the entire floor. But we could come and go as we pleased. No guards, we simply were required to report for work on time each day. When our new barracks were finished, it was much better. Buses then took us to and from work. Before, at the boarding house, we had to ride city buses. And our new building was brand new! My family asked if I was ever late coming home to the barracks, and I can truthfully say we had some close calls, but no AWOLs.

While I was stationed at the Naval Supply Base in Oakland, I heard that the USS Hornet, the aircraft carrier, was in San Francisco for repairs after suffering damage from a typhoon. I wanted to see this big ship my husband-to-be had been stationed on. His squadron attached to the ship had played a major part in our fight against the Japanese.

Three other WAVES and I took the water taxi across the Bay to where the carrier was moored. It was August 1945 and the War was just about over. Many of the personnel regularly assigned to the ship were not there. All the planes and personnel who worked with them had been removed. When we saw the Marine guarding the gangplank we told him we only hoped to see the ship. He said we could come aboard with him as an escort.

We soon found ourselves being escorted into the galley where huge tubs of meat, pickles and cheese were the source of some sandwiches for us. After finishing our sandwiches, we listened to Taps played while we stood on the fantail of the hangar deck.

I shall always remember listening to that bugle while we stood at attention on the carrier's deck.

****

I was discharged from the WAVES in April 1946, and married James Hampton the next month. My long-suffering husband of currently 58 years was also in the Navy when we met. He saw duty on the USS Lexington in the Battle of the Coral Sea. We have lived all around the West, including California, New Mexico, Idaho and finally La Pine, Oregon, where we settled in 1983. We have four daughters, nine grandkids and two great-grandkids. I have worked in various clerical jobs at different times. But the job I enjoy most is homemaker/gardener/needlecrafter.

Chapter Twelve

ABLE, BAKER, CHARLIE, DOG ....
Nancy Underwood Wachsnicht, MARINE

On a stormy winter night in a small town, Brooks, Alberta, Canada, a small girl came into this world. The name of Nan Leigh Ward was entered on a birth certificate. After a few months the mother decided she didn't like that name so it was changed to Nancy Eletha. Unfortunately, it was not changed on the birth certificate.

Why bring up the subject of a birth certificate? It became a problem in March 1943, when for no logical reason, I decided to enlist in the Marine Corps. The enlisting officer told me that I would need to submit my birth certificate.

This is a problem you see. Not only is the name wrong, it also says I was born in Canada. You have to be a citizen of the United States to enlist in the service.

I hoped Mother would help me with this; however, I was reluctant to approach her on the subject. How would she react to having her only child in the service? With some anxiety I went to her and asked if she could prove that I was a citizen of the United States. When I told her why I needed proof of citizenship, her eyes got round as dollars and tears formed. Good heavens! I didn't think it would be that bad. Surprise! She wasn't unhappy, she was delighted. She just wished she was young enough to go with me.

"You will have no problem," she told me. "When I got my papers you came in on mine. You have a letter from the Immigration Office stating you are a citizen."

I was enlisted. A couple of weeks later I received orders to report to Hunter College, New York. A couple of days before the scheduled departure for Hunter College I received orders changing the destination to Camp Lejeune, North Carolina.

I boarded a train in Portland, Oregon, and headed for Chicago. In Chicago all of the women who were headed for Camp Lejeune were conducted to another section of the station where we were to board something that vaguely resembled a train. It had the appearance of a boxcar with windows. It had uncomfortable, hard seats, no air conditioning, windows that could be raised. However, if the windows were raised you got wind, dust and bugs.

We arrived in Richmond, Virginia, starved, dehydrated, dirty and sweaty. We were detrained and marched to a large dining room in a nearby hotel. What a marvelous change. It was cool, clean and the food was plentiful and very good. I had my first taste of grits.

When we arrived at Camp Lejeune I was so tired and groggy I remember very little of what took place on our arrival. I know that at some time we were issued a blanket, sheets, pillow and case, towels and soap. We were assigned a bunk in a barracks room and given instructions on how to properly make up our bunk. You had to be able to bounce a quarter on it when it was properly made.

Now we were introduced to our first meal in the mess hall, or would you rather call it chow hall. Either nomenclature is appropriate. Would you rather eat mess or chow?

Next day we were issued uniforms. Each woman was individually fitted in her uniform. We had received instructions when we received our orders that we were to provide our own underwear, stockings and night wear.

Early each morning we fell out for exercise. Then we had breakfast, then drill, more food and in the afternoon we attended various classes. Somewhere in this time period we were marched to the dispensary and given a number of shots. Guess what! The shots made me sicker than a dog. I ended up in the dispensary for a few days.

Strange, we were marched down to the river and shown landing barges. We were marched on board, taken out in the river, then back to shore and disembarked. This seemed so useless; we didn't need this training as we weren't going into combat. What is even stranger, we never had any training in firearms. We were taught the proper use of gas masks.

After evening chow we were free to do whatever we wanted. By that time of day all I wanted was a shower and all the sack time I could get.

We had four weeks of basic training. We were rushed through as quickly as possible so that we could assume our assigned duties. The primary reason women were enlisted was to fill office and non-combatant duties as soon as possible so that men could be shipped to the Pacific Front. At that time our country was in the midst of taking back the Pacific Islands from the Japanese.

Funny little things stick in your mind. I remember close order drill. Because I was rather short I was always near the back of the line. The girl who marched behind me was always stepping on my heels. She had my shoes pretty well worn on the back. Sometimes my shoe almost came off when she stepped on it. It is difficult to march with your shoe half off your foot.

One of the highlights of camp life was mail call. Those boxes from home were greatly appreciated. Everyone was good about sharing. One of the most special gifts for me came just before Christmas. Mother sent a fir tree. It was small, about 2-3 feet tall. There was a stand to put it in and lots of pretty ornaments. No lights, as that wouldn't have been practical. Our barracks room was the only one with Christmas decoration. A real live tree .... a fir tree from Oregon!

Upon completion of basic training, though some women were shipped to California, I elected to remain in North Carolina and was assigned to Communication Center. At the time we women were assigned our duties, there were twenty-two men manning the Center. Ten women replaced those twenty-two men. The Center operated 24 hours a day, 7 days a week. This meant we pulled some very long consecutive duty hours. Two women were assigned to man the Center over the weekends. We would be excused at 4 p.m. Friday afternoon, go to our barracks, change into dungarees, pick up a blanket and pillow and some food, then report back to duty at 5 p.m. to work until 9 a.m. Monday morning.

I loved the Monday mornings after weekend duty because we got to go to the chow hall at a time when it was too late for breakfast and too early for lunch. We got special treatment. It was not unusual to get steak for breakfast. It was also the time when the fresh bread and pies came out of the oven. Believe me, two of us could do away with a pie and a pot of coffee with no trouble.

One incident that sticks in my memory of weekend duties was a night when I had to call our captain in to decode Top Secret messages. I, as a non-commissioned personnel, could not handle Top Secret code. When he had finished his work, he came out of his office and asked what we were having for dinner. I reached into my desk drawer and took out a couple of packages.

"Would you like K rations or C rations? The apples are a little old and dried up but better than nothing," I said to him. He stared at me for a short time and said, "Is this some kind of a joke?"

"No, Sir," I replied.

"Are you telling me this is your usual meal when you have the night duty?" he asked.

"Yes, Sir, this is our usual fare," I replied.

He turned around and went back into his office. A half hour later there was a knock on the door. When I opened it there stood a sergeant with two paper bags in his arms. "Here you are, enjoy," he said.

In those bags were hot steak sandwiches, salad, fresh fruit, an apple pie and a thermos of coffee. Man, what a treat! It has come from the Service Battalion which had the best chow hall on the base. From that time on all personnel on night duty had hot meals delivered.

I remember a Thanksgiving when I pulled duty and we had dinner at that chow hall. It was a traditional Thanksgiving meal with all of the trimmings, even mince pie and pumpkin pie. As I was getting nicely going on this feast, a corpsman wearing an apron approached our table. He reached under his apron and brought out a couple of bottles of beer. Cold beer! How's that for living it up?

The Communication Center not only sent and received radio messages, we also handled the Camp mail. We gathered and delivered mail to various building on the base. One of the most exasperating deliveries was the mail that went form our headquarters building to another administrative building located about a half mile away. This delivery was made on a motor scooter. Here's the problem. We girls wore skirts and silly little caps that were hard to keep on our heads even when we weren't moving. The scooter had to be driven and the mail had to be carried. You see, we needed one hand to hold down our skirt, one hand to hold onto our hat, one hand to drive the scooter and two hands to carry the mail.

I took this frustrating problem to our Captain. He told me that if I could submit to him a satisfactory delivery route using the three delivery trucks we had, he would give permission to abolish the scooter. It took me less than an hour to come up with a far more satisfactory delivery system.

Speaking of trucks, our trucks in those days did not

have adjustable seats or tilt steering wheels. Being about 5'2", I had difficulty seeing over the steering wheel. Furthermore, my legs were too short to reach the brake and gas pedals comfortably. I lucked out. Because I was in charge of scheduling the mail deliveries, I used this opportunity to assign the truck driving duties to the taller girls.

After completion of basic training and being assigned to our duties, we got to take our first liberty. Going off base was an eye opening experience. Most of us recruits were from the west coast, mostly from the Northwest. Segregation was something I had read about and heard about but had never experienced. At home I knew our colored family well. They were the same as anyone else. In fact, I frequently rode to school on the handle bars of Lawrence's bicycle.

All spruced in uniform, I got on a bus and took a seat by the window near the back of the bus. A colored woman walked down the aisle and stopped by me. She said, "Honey, you'all cain't sit there." To which I responded, "Why not, this seat was vacant."

"Honey, only us coloreds can ride in the back of the bus," was her reply.

I moved, but made up my mind that this was pretty silly and something was going to be done about it! The next time on liberty a group of us girls got our heads together and decided we didn't approve of segregation and we weren't going to put up with it. Next time out on liberty, each of us took a seat by a window in every row from the front to the back of the bus. Those poor colored people didn't know what to do. We asked them to sit by us. Some of them did, reluctantly. Others stood up all the way to town. We also stood in the line with colored people to buy our bus tickets. It took a few months but they finally gave up and sat wherever there was a vacant seat, as long as it was a bus to and from the base.

On a trip to New Bern, my bunkie Helga and I were having a great time just wandering around the city sightseeing. We saw a small colored man carrying a basket full of paper bags and calling out "Goobers for sale, goobers for sale." I turned to Helga and said, "What is a goober?" She shrugged her shoulders and replied, "How do I know. Let's buy some and find out." We bought a bag and continued on down the street. Finally she said, "Well, let's see what we bought." We opened the bag and in unison exclaimed, "Peanuts!"

I found their speech a little different, not only their southern drawl, but also their words. I had a hard time to keep from laughing one time when a boy asked if he could "carry me" to dinner. I guessed he was asking to "take me" to dinner. Thank goodness I minded my manners and accepted politely.

The local families often invited service people to their homes for Sunday dinner. Some of the homes were very lovely. It was great to get to taste and enjoy southern cooking. I will say, their Virginia cured ham is every bit as good as they brag about. On one of these Sundays the family informed me that they were taking me for a drive after dinner. They wanted me to see their beautiful mountains. Well, we drove and drove. I kept wondering how far away the mountains were. At last the woman said, "Aren't you enjoying our mountains? You haven't said a word."

A light went on in my brain. Good heavens, we must be in the mountains. Quickly I said, "Oh yes! I am absolutely speechless." Compared to what I was used to, these weren't even decent mole hills, but I decided diplomacy was proper at that moment.

In North Carolina the area between New River and the Atlantic Ocean has a lot of swamp area. We were warned to keep to the paved roads, never to wander into the swampy areas. They are filled with snakes, many of which are poisonous. And mosquitoes are a very uncomfortable problem. The one night I pulled guard duty I thought I was being eaten alive. I asked myself, why do people live in places like this?

One Sunday afternoon a girl and I took a canoe out into the river for a cruise. Do you cruise with canoes, or just go paddling? Anyway, we got tired of paddling and just drifted for awhile. It was a beautiful day and we were really enjoying the scenery. The greenery along the river there was quite different than our Pacific Northwest. As time was moving along, it was getting time to get back to the base. I took my paddle and pushed against what I thought was a log. Whoops! The log rolled over and opened a huge mouth. We got our introduction to a live alligator! You wouldn't believe how fast two people could move those paddles. We were in high gear in 30 seconds flat.

I found the people of the South to be very friendly and outgoing. One day I stopped at a tobacco farm, never having seen tobacco grow before. The man explained the growing, harvesting and curing. It is quite a process, and that was very educational. Another experience I had was one afternoon as I was driving around a small town. I was in the outskirts when I noticed a nicely kept place. There was a yard, no grass but nicely swept. This was surrounded by a picket fence, unpainted but in good condition. The house was wooden, unpainted but it was very clean. An older colored woman was sitting in a rocking chair on the front porch shelling peas. I decided to stop and talk to her. As I approached the porch she rose and greeted me with a big smile. We introduced ourselves and she asked me to have a seat. "I just had to stop and say how much I like the way you keep your place so neat and clean looking," I told her.

She thanked me and asked where I was from. When I told her I was from clear across the continent and lived in a completely different climate, she was really thrilled to meet someone from so far away. She thought it was wonderful that I would stop and call on her. About a half hour went by, then I said I'd better be going.

"Oh, you all cain't go yet," she said. "I just picked some ripe peaches out of my back yard, and I would love to have you stay and have a bite." She fixed a lovely repast. Not only did she have a couple of trees in her back yard, she had a garden, chickens and a cow. So it was scones, fresh peaches and whipped cream she served. Aren't people wonderful? They are gracious and outgoing when given a chance.

The next event in my tour of duty was my two week furlough, a trip back home. Helga and I planned our furloughs at the same time so we could travel together. She was going to Washington and I to Oregon. The train going north out of

Wilmington was packed. Over-packed! Rather than lose any time from our vacation, however, we elected to crowd on. We tried standing in the aisle. That didn't last long. We soon joined many others sitting on the floor.

As usual in those times, we were filthy, dirty and uncomfortable when we arrived in Chicago. I asked a Shore Patrol if he knew if there was a YWCA near by where we could get a shower. He said he would make some inquiries for us, just to stand by. He returned saying there was no YWCA, but there was a YMCA and he made arrangements for someone to take us there. The shower room at the YMCA was emptied just for the two of us. We were given towels and soap and told to take our time. You never know what you can get until you ask for it, do you.

That journey is full of memories. When we arrived in St. Paul it was around midnight and we were both hungry and thirsty. We were told there was a USO in the train station with coffee and doughnuts. Helga said she would watch our belongings while I went for treats. I was the only woman in line, but remember, I was in uniform like the men. When I got to the counter, the woman who was serving gave me a sneer and said, "Move along, this is for service men only."

It was quite a shock to get this kind of treatment but I did as I was told and moved on. I went back to my seat and told Helga what had happened. "Guess we are out of luck. We'll just have to get along without treats," I remarked. But I was wrong. When the train started moving, through the door came the biggest Shore Patrol I have ever seen. He handed me a paper bag. "Here's your doughnuts and coffee. I saw and heard what was said at that booth. That woman will never work there again. Have a good trip."

We were riding on a Navy troop train carrying sailors to a training base either in Idaho or Utah. For us to get into the dining car we had to pass through four cars full of sailors. Can you imagine what it was like for two female Marines to pass though this sea of sailors? We finally did get there and back, but the next time we heard dinner call we just sat very quietly. We told the conductor we would rather be hungry than go through that fiasco again. A short time later he came back accompanied by two Shore Patrol. They escorted us to the dining car and back, so from then on meals were not so bad.

Furlough was wonderful, those few days at home. It was interesting to see that civilians also had their limitations. Many of the things I took for granted before the war were no longer available. Sugar was rationed. Imagine living on a farm with all of that fruit to can, and no sugar! Mother had a whole new cookbook of recipes that used honey instead of sugar. She made her own soap. Whenever she fried bacon she would save the fat and pour it into a container to be strained and processed for soap. It is amazing how much bacon you use on a farm, so there was plenty of soap! When furlough was up I was fortunate to be able to fly back to my base instead of having another long train ride.

At this time the United States was in the process of taking back the South Pacific islands from the Japanese. Fighting was fierce, casualties were high. Many of the Marines who had been through the invasions were returned to Camp Lejeune for R & R. Many were badly in need of medical attention. Malaria and coral fever were the most prevalent afflictions, coral fever being caused by contact with the reefs as the men were landing during the invasion process.

One evening when I was on night duty in the Communications Center, a female Marine 2nd lieutenant brought me a message to send. The message stated that there was going to be a going-away party for the First Marine Battalion who would be departing for the South Pacific on May 10th. It said to come and wish your comrades well as they depart for Luzon. I read the message, handed it back to her and stated, "I will not send this message; it would be a breach of security."

"Who do you think you are?" she asked. "Since when does a PFC think she can defy an order from a Lieutenant? I am putting you on report for insubordination if you do not send this."

"I am not sending this message. If you wish to charge me with insubordination that is fine with me." The following morning there was a report citing my insubordination on the captain's desk. I was called in and questioned on the happenings of the prior night. When I cited my case for the message being a breach of security about when or where our troops are being sent, the captain smiled and said, "You are to be commended for your action. The lieutenant, not you, will receive the reprimand."

The humid weather in that part of the country is something I had never experienced. With the temperature in the 90s and 100s, it was very uncomfortable. Whenever I was where I could get to my squad room I would rush in, grab some dry clothes, take a shower and put on dry clothes. Taking a towel to dry off was a waste of time--you could never get dry!

And the weather played tricks with our clothing, too. Our summer uniforms were green and white striped seersucker, two-piece dresses. The first issue material was much nicer than what was issued later on. One of my favorite dresses was so bleached out from being washed and worn in the sun, it was nearly all white. I was on liberty on hot Saturday when disaster struck. My top ripped from collar line to the hem line. What can be done in a situation like this? Just hurry back to the base in the best way possible.

Our barracks were two story buildings with hardwood floors which were waxed and polished to the nth degree. On my way to work one morning, just as I got to the head of the stairs, another girl came rushing up and bumped into me. My feet slid on the waxed floors and I went down the stairs end over end. At the bottom, girls rushed to me and checked me over. No blood was visible and I didn't feel like I was broke anywhere, so we proceeded to go to work. At work I noticed that one of my legs was hurting so I pulled up my skirt and sure enough, there was quite a gash caused by the metal fastener that held up my stocking. At sick bay a young corpsman came to help me. When I raised my skirt he got red as a beet and didn't seem to know what to do. I suggested that just some disinfectant and a Band-Aid would probably take care of the injury.

A day later I found that I was hurt worse than I thought. I was getting dizzy spells and having an awful headache. Aspirin did nothing for me. One day, after getting off duty, I went back to the barracks, removed my uniform and laid down on my bunk. I did not feel like going for chow. The next time I opened my eyes I found I was in the hospital. I had lost consciousness. Many tests were conducted to determine the cause of my blackouts. At that time it never occurred to me to mention that I had fallen down a complete flight of stairs.

I was shipped from Camp Lejeune Hospital to Bethesda Hospital in Maryland for three or four more months of testing. Since nothing could be found, I would be discharged from the service on a medical disability. What was so heartbreaking about that was that I had just applied for a transfer to Honolulu. Too bad, that was no longer possible.

For the final few months I was put up in a barracks in Arlington, Virginia. When I arrived, snow was on the ground, but within a month spring arrived with an array of flowers that was spectacular.

Being in uniform I could go anywhere without cost. We could ride the buses, enter the art galleries, see all of the monuments at our own leisure. I saw the outside of the Capital, but never had a tour inside. Washington, D.C. is a place every citizen should see at some time in their life.

So my tour of duty ended, and I returned home. I went into the service in good shape, and came out in very bad condition. I was skin and bones, had terrible headaches and didn't feel like doing much of anything. Fortunately, our family doctor recognized my problem immediately. The X-rays showed that my spine was badly mis-aligned and was causing nerve damage. If I moved wrong , it would pinch my nerves and cause me to black out. It took close to three years of therapy before my spine would stay in place and allow me to function properly.

After I recuperated enough, I went into Civil Service, working for the Corps of Engineers during the Korean conflict. We were shipping supplies to our troops in Korea. I spent the years from 1950 through 1974 in government service.

A tour of military duty is such a marvelous opportunity to grow and enlarge one's knowledge, and appreciation of people. I attended a conference one time where the main speaker said, "You are what you are because of where you were, when." It took me a few days to thoroughly digest this statement. It changed my way of viewing life. I realized what a great opportunity each of us has to grow in and appreciate this life God has given us. It made me wonder about how a country this vast and diverse can operate and become a great nation. Perhaps this is what makes us so great. I know it has made life easier for me to accept and appreciate other people for what they are, not what I think they should be. It is marvelous that I can be unique in my own way, and you can do pretty much what suits you and we do not interfere with each other. I can thank my military service for much of this personal growth.

****

After WWII I married an Army man, and we had 49 happy years of marriage. As we had no children, after my 25 years of work in civilian service, I found time to do many of the things I never had time for when working. I have been quite active in the American Legion. In 2003 I was elected the first woman commander of Albany Post 10, American Legion. Albany is the largest Legion Post in Oregon. Another honor I received was in March 2004 when I was presented, as a representative of the US Marine Corps, a Non-commissioned Officers Association of America World War II Medallion by Governor Ted Kulongoski.

MARINE Nancy Wachsnicht, pictured between Governor Kulongoski and Walter Crews, NCOA member, displays her Medallion.

In March 2004, Oregon's Governor Theodore Kulongoski presented eleven World War II veterans with World War II Medallions. The Medallions were created by the Non Commissioned Officers' Association of America as a way to honor the military men and women of WWII who stood tall for America during the dark hours of the war. Medallion recipients are among a generation of veterans who made a tremendous sacrifice to their State and Nation--a generation referred to as the "Greatest Generation."

Chapter Thirteen

A Storekeeper's Store of Memories

Nellie Sauter Sorensen, WAVE

I was born May 22, 1923 in Lyle, Washington and grew up on a farm along the Columbia River. My parents raised produce and shipped it to Portland on the train. Dad fished commercially on the Columbia River; sheep were raised and sold as well as chickens and eggs.

I had 5 siblings, 2 older brothers and 3 younger--a sister and two brothers. I attended Balch Grade School and graduated from White Salmon High School in 1939. Following my high school years, I worked on the family farm helping Dad fish. That was until 1943 when I decided that with my two older brothers in the Navy, I wanted to join the WAVES.

On July 23, 1943 I went to Portland, Oregon, where I took my aptitude test and physical and was sworn into the WAVES that same afternoon. I then had a long talk with the WAVE officer concerning ratings and rating requirements and what to take with me when I went to boot camp at Hunter College, New York City. I arrived home about midnight, very happy and excited.

About a week later I received my orders. I was to leave home on Sunday night, August 8th and would arrive in New York City on August 12th. It was just as though I were dreaming. The time passed very fast and soon I was on the train, feeling very much alone...sad about leaving, but very excited about the new and different life ahead of me.

At 8:00 the next morning, the train was leaving Spokane, Washington, headed east. All that first day there were no other girls on the train going to boot camp, but during the night 3 more got on in Montana and we got acquainted the next day. We had all been hoping to meet someone else, as we had all started out alone. We stayed together the rest of the trip.

On Wednesday morning, August 11th, we arrived in Chicago and had only time to change stations and catch our train to New York. On this train we met about 15 or 20 girls from Washington and Montana on their way to Hunter, and we really had a wonderful time. Practically every stop the train made, more girls got on. So by the time it reached New York City, there were between 75 and 100 of us.

We arrived at Grand Central Station on Thursday morning, August 12th, and were met by officers and specialists from the training school at Hunter College. We had breakfast at the station, then went by subway to the armory where we were assigned our quarters and got our first Navy hats. It was the first time most of us had ridden in a subway, and we didn't enjoy it. We then formed groups and marched to the building where we were to live for the next month.

Building E, Apartment S-51--that's where I was assigned. When I got there none of my roommates had arrived so I looked around for a few minutes waiting for them. There were 4 rooms to the apartment, 2 of which were

Left to right, the "office gang" - Jane Gearey, Sarah Tiktinsky, Nellie Sauter (Sorensen) Lillian Fisher

used as bunkrooms--4 bunks in each--and the kitchen, which was used to wash and dry our clothes only--and the bathroom to be shared by 8 girls. My roommates were Penny Parriots and Rita Lewis of Cleveland, Ohio, and Nadine (Deannie) Minetree of Hopkinsville, Kentucky.

Friday the 13th we had our physicals and that was followed by many busy days filled with aptitude tests, lectures, drills, shots, uniform fittings and finally that happy day for all of us when we first put on our uniforms and packed our civilian clothes to send them home. Regiment 12 was a very proud group when our first Regimental Review was held, especially Company 7 as we had been chosen to act as Color Company. Our 2nd Review was held inside on one of those hot, rainy summer days. Then came interviews and, last but not least, posting of lists of where we were being sent.

Deannie and Penny were going to yeoman's School at Stillwater, Oklahoma, and Rita and I to storekeeper school in Milledgeville, Georgia.

Our last weekend at Hunter we had shore liberty on Saturday and Sunday afternoon. Two of Rita's friends were in New York from Cleveland and we spent part of our time with them. We visited Rockefeller Center, St. Patrick's Cathedral and a few other places. Then Deannie and I went to the Statue of Liberty. It was a long time before we reached the top, or at least it seemed so. Coming down was worse, as you could see all the way down.

On September 9th we left Hunter and were on our way to Georgia. On the train I met Eleanor Young from California, who later was my roommate and one of the best friends I've ever had. We arrived in Milledgeville about 0600 on September 11th and marched from the station to Ennis Hall where we were to live for the next three months.

The training school was on the campus of the Georgia State College for Women and the Navy was using part of the

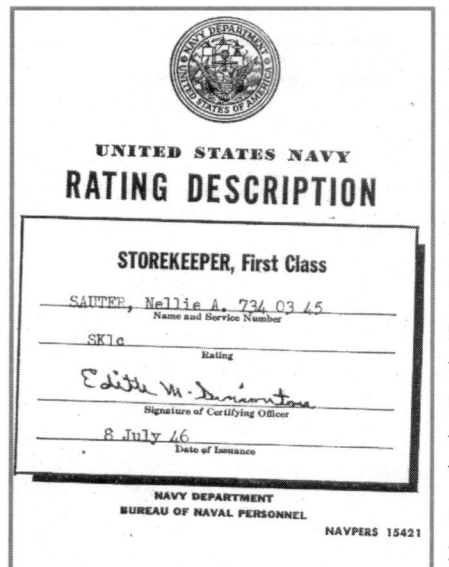

UNITED STATES NAVY
RATING DESCRIPTION

STOREKEEPER, First Class

SAUTER, Nellie A. 734 03 45
Name and Service Number

SK1c
Rating

Edith M. Dumonton
Signature of Certifying Officer

8 July 46
Date of Issuance

NAVY DEPARTMENT
BUREAU OF NAVAL PERSONNEL

NAVPERS 15421

college buildings. We ate in the regular college dining room. That first morning was wonderful, a very nice change from the trays and hurried lines at Hunter. Here we all entered the dining room and remained standing until we were seated by the Officer of the Day. The food was on the tables when we entered and we sat 8 at a table; if more food was wanted, we went to the kitchen for it. When we finished eating, we stacked the dishes and remained seated until we were dismissed.

My roommates were a swell trio. Roberta (Bobby) Rogers of California; Frances Radcliff from Ohio, and Katherine Saunders of Iowa. Bobby and I were practically inseparable for the first 2 months. Our first weekend liberty we spent in Macon, though most of our time was spent at Cochran Field as the air cadets we knew were restricted to the field that weekend! Our second weekend liberty, Eleanor and I went to Atlanta and had a nice time.

We graduated from Milledgeville the last of November and most of the girls went home before going to their new station. Eleanor and I were among the few whose homes were too far away to visit in the time we had, so we went directly to Washington, D.C.

The first night in D.C. we were sent to the Receiving Station at Anacastia, then the next morning we marched to the Roosevelt Hotel. We spent 10 days at the Hotel and lived in a beautiful suite along with 3 other girls. During these first days we spent quite a bit of time walking around Washington with a map so that we could find any place we wanted to go. We reported for work on December 2nd but had plenty of time in the evenings to get acquainted with the city.

We then moved to Florida Hall, Arlington Farms, Virginia. This was a large housing project across the Potomac from Washington. Three of the halls were WAVE quarters and the other 7 were halls for the civilian government girls. The civilian halls were made with all private rooms; the WAVE quarters had cubicles with 2 girls in each, 50 girls in each wing. One of my roommates from Georgia, Kathy, was also in Florida Hall. The other two had been sent to Pensacola, Florida. Also, Rita was there and I soon learned that Deannie and Penny had both been sent to D.C. from yeoman School and were right here in Florida Hall.

Eleanor was my roommate for a little over a year and we had some wonderful times. We spent many hours seeing interesting places in and around Washington, including the Smithsonian Institute, National History Museum, Library of Congress, Art Galleries, Washington Monument, Jefferson and Lincoln Memorials, Mt. Vernon, Lee Mansion, Arlington National Cemetery, the Tomb of the Unknown Soldier, the Amphitheater and many other places when off duty.

In December 1944, Eleanor left for Shoemaker, California, and from there for Hawaii. In the next few months I had several roommates. Then June Dedrick moved in and stayed for almost a year. We had some swell times together. The whole group of F-Wing was fun and we had some wonderful times in the smoker, taking pictures, eating and just acting up.

In March of 1944 I had met my brother Frank in New York City one weekend and had met his friend Ester Matson. I spent many weekends with her between then and the time I was discharged in July 1946 and had a wonderful time with her and her friends.

I was home for 6 days in June 1944, in May 1945 for 10 days, and then in April 1946 for 16 days. All these trips home were wonderful because I went a different route each time.

In 1945 Ruth Dumphy and Ethel Anderson and I went to the Watergate concerts during the summer, and to operettas, plays and concerts, as well as an opera.

For Christmas that year we had four days off. We left Washington for Rochester, riding on the platform between the cars on the train. We were lucky as there were many who couldn't even get on the train. After quite a few stops there finally was room enough for us to get inside and sit on our suitcases. When we changed trains, the other train was already full so about 30 of us rode in a baggage car for several hours. We changed trains again and for the last 45 minutes of our trip we had a seat. Our trip back was uneventful as we left Rochester at 0630 Christmas morning and spent all day traveling. We slept part of the way back as we had stayed up all the night before. We decorated the tree in the afternoon, spent part of the evening taking pictures, went to midnight mass. Then it was time to leave for the train. It was one Christmas that has been long remembered!

By January I was scheduled to be discharged some time in February. But after much consideration of the matter, I decided to stay in until September 1st. So I signed over and made 1st class storekeeper. However, when the matter of signing over until July 1946 came up, I thought about it but decided definitely against it. Both Ruthie and Andy signed to stay in.

On July 3rd, a group of us who were being discharged in the next couple of weeks and who had lived in F-Wing for quite some time, had a farewell party. On the 5th the first of the group left for home, and Stella Swick and I reported to the Separation Center. We received our discharges on July 8th at noon and went out to spend the afternoon shopping for civilian clothes. I decided not to go home immediately. Instead, I went to Hopkinsville, Kentucky, to spend a week with my good friend Deannie, her 1½ -year-old son and the rest of her family.

****

Once I returned home to Washington, I picked up where I'd left off and continued helping Dad fish and take care of the gardening.

While I was home on leave in 1945, I'd met a friend's brother, Kenneth Sorensen. We had gone our own ways, I back to Washington, D.C. and he to Okinawa with the Army. We met up again in September 1946 and began dating.

On February 22, 1947, we were married and moved onto the family farm in Hartland (now known as High Prairie). We had five children: Linda (September 1947); Sharon (March 1949); Kenneth Michael (August 1948); Martin(October 1952)) and Leroy (May 1954).

Our family was very busy over the years. After farming, we owned a grocery/locker/meat cutting business, then a tavern which we finally sold in 1982. All the training and experience I received from the WAVES storekeeper specialty provided me with the knowledge necessary to operate the businesses we had efficiently and effectively.

I have stayed in touch with my WAVE roommate Deannie (Nadine Minetree Warren) over the years and clear across the continent. That has truly been a lasting Navy friendship.

Since February 2004 I have been a resident of the Oregon Veterans Home in The Dalles, Oregon.

Intelligence Meant Tight Lips!

Nadine Minetree Warren, WAVE

I entered boot camp at Hunter College in New York City in August of 1943. I was in the 12th Regiment, which finished training in September. One of my roommates was Nellie Sauter (now Sorensen) who became a special friend. Her help was something I couldn't get along without. My problem was that I was way too short to climb up into the upper bunk where I was assigned. And the Navy didn't want any trading around. So Nellie would hoist me up every night and help me down in the morning. She was my ladder. Nellie also had to tie my tie to try to make sure I was in "ship shape".

Nadine Minetree and Nellie Sauter, boot camp roommates, beginning a 50-year friendship.

Wartime parade, including WAVES from their storekeeper school training, in downtown Stillwater, Oklahoma, 1943.

During wartime "Emergency Status," the military men or women could never be out of uniform. So back home on the farm, the challenge was obvious for the ladies.

But I still received 5 demerits for having a run in my stocking. As punishment I was given the job of cleaning out the smokers--and I didn't smoke.

From boot I was sent to Yeoman school in Stillwater, Oklahoma, at Oklahoma A & M. My first shore leave came in October followed by a leave to go home for a short visit. It was on that leave that I made an amusing discovery: a Navy uniform is not the proper dress for riding horseback. In fact, I'm not too sure how I was able to get on my horse without Nellie there to hoist me up. Graduation from Stillwater came in December.

My assignment after training was to work in the main Navy Department in the office of Navy Intelligence, or A-7 as we were known, under Commander E. Bartlett. We were schooled to never reveal anything we did on the job.

Intelligence was a very important factor during WWII, as was the security surrounding it. I was discharged in 1945.

There were four of us WAVES who became fast friends in boot camp, among them Marian Banks, Nellie Sauter and Barbara, whose last name I've forgotten. Both she and Marian have passed away. For many years I stayed in contact with all three, and have stayed in contact with Nellie over the many years in between. I talk to her occasionally where she lives in the Veterans Home in Oregon.

Second anniversary of the Women Accepted for Volunteer Emergency Service. A total of 9,999 WAVES viewed from the top of the Washington Monument, 30 July 1944.

****

In 1944, I married my civilian sweetheart, and had our first son in 1945, the second in 1950 and the third son in 1951. After 49 years of marriage, my husband passed away, and I lost two of our sons to accidents. Hard as it was to do, I finally sold our family home in Hopkinsville, Kentucky. It was very difficult to leave the place I had grown up in, married and raised a family in. I moved to Danville, Virginia, to be near my remaining son, Don Warren. I have had some health problems, but still drive and am thankful for my 81 ½ years of life.

Chapter Fifteen

DO YOU HAVE MY INITIALS ON YOUR FILLINGS?

Genevieve (Jean) Sobolewski Olterzewski, WAAC/WAC

In the summer of 1942, I was engaged to Sergeant Russell Harshbarger. He was stationed at Fort Dix, New Jersey, with the Rangers. His Company was sent to Africa to fight the Germans. On November 8th he was shot, and he died in the hospital on the 10th. His family and I received the news of his death the week before Christmas. My life and that of his family was very sad.

During the early part of 1943, I began to see many signs that said women were needed in the Army. At that time I was working at Conmar, a zipper manufacturer in Newark, New Jersey. So in March of 1943, I enlisted in the Army. My employer had Army contracts and guaranteed my job upon my return from the service.

I was called to active duty in early April and was stationed at Fort Oglethorpe, Georgia for training in the Women's Army Auxiliary Corps (WAAC). While in military training, we marched in review before President Franklin D. Roosevelt. That was a great day for the WAACs!

After weeks of training, I was sent to Buckingham Army Air Field (BAAF) in Fort Myers, Florida. It was a large training center for pilots, co-pilots, bombardiers and gunners. The WAACs were permanent party. I was assigned to the hospital laboratory where I was the lone WAAC with five men. (The Air Force sent me to Atlanta, Georgia, long enough to learn how to run various blood tests that doctors would order for the patients.) I would go to all the wards, draw the blood from the patients, and take it back to the lab for the different tests to be run.

Fort Myers was a small town. There were three hotels, one movie theatre, one Catholic Church and one drugstore. Lots of GIs used to hang around on the corner at the drugstore. One day I was passing by the drugstore with my good friend and fellow WAAC Elsie Libes when someone called out to me, "Hey, Jean, don't you know me anymore?" He was a former patient. I took a look back and then recognized him and shouted back, "Hello, Jack. I didn't recognize you with

Jean   Elsie   Elsie   Jean

your clothes on...I mean, ...you look so different in your pajamas ... I mean..." With all the GIs standing there laughing their heads off, Elsie grabbed me by the elbow and got me out of there!

While I was home on my first leave, my younger sister Wanda told me she had signed up for the WAACs also and was waiting for her orders to report for duty. Wanda was ultimately stationed at Lowry Field, Denver, Colorado. She worked in the hospital there as a nurse's aide. A few months after that my youngest brother, George, left high school to join the paratroopers.

In 1945 I met Bruce, who was in training at BAAF to be a bombardier. We dated often while at our field. When he was preparing to transfer, he had to have a dental check-up. At that time I was working as a dental technician. I was really angry with him at the moment--don't remember why. Told the captain that the next person I bring in for a check-up is my EX-boyfriend. The Captain said, "I'll fix it so he'll never forget you. When I put the fillings in his teeth, I'll carve your initials in them!" He didn't really do it--I don't think. And then again, maybe he did!

Bruce and I continued our friendship by letter writing. In one letter he asked me to send some pictures of myself. I sent him a picture of me at the beach in a bathing suit and got a fast reply to my letter. He wrote, "Whatcha trying to do, get me to go AWOL?" Our friendship lasted way beyond the service, by his keeping track of me even when he had three kids and I had five! During the time we were corresponding he proposed to me two or three times, but I just couldn't see myself living in Louisiana.

One day I was "on the carpet" before the CO. The MPs had turned my name in for being out with an officer. The CO said, "Don't you know you are not allowed to go out with officers?" "Yes, M'am," I replied. "Well, why did you do it?" she asked. "Well, M'am," I answered, "He was SO cute and he asked me SO nice, I COULDN'T say no." The CO threw both her hands up to her face in surprise. I had to wash windows in the dayroom of our barracks as punishment.

After the service I returned to work for my pre-war employer, and life carried on. Many of my WAC friends would stop by New Jersey for visits. Eve came from Montana, Natalie from Texas, Sophie from New York. Virginia would visit from Florida, Elizabeth "MacKenzie" would come up from Philadelphia, and Elsie Libes from North Carolina. I traveled to visit with my good friend Elsie (now Boyer) several times over the years. In fact, Elsie and I made it a point to be at the dedication of the Women's Memorial in Washington, D.C. That evening at dinner we met General Colin Powell. He was interesting and very nice. I'm glad to have had the opportunity to talk with him.

My sister Wanda suffered from multiple sclerosis and spent 10 years in the Veterans' Nursing Home in Paramus, New Jersey. While I was visiting with her one day, General Carol Mutter, a three-star General in the US Marines, was at the nursing home presenting certificates for women in military service. My sister was very proud and honored to receive her certificate of service.

During a local Veterans' Day ceremony, I spoke with a Navy officer and told her I had been in the WACs in WWII. She remarked, "Thanks to people like you, you made it easier for people like me who followed after." On another occasion, a young soldier, a very young soldier, was at a town function. I mentioned to him that my husband had been in the Seabees, and I had been in the WACs during WWII. He replied, "I thought everyone in WWII already died."

****

I met my husband, Joseph, a few years after the War. He had been in the Navy Seabees. I was 32 at the time we were married. My husband was 25. By the summer of 1958 we had four daughters and one son. Now we have an additional 8 grandchildren and 3 great-grandchildren. Life is great! Joe and I have been married 53 years and we're still in love! I am now 83 years young. I belong to a few senior citizens clubs as well as the American Legion. Through the AARP club we work to help homeless children by collecting and donating stuffed teddy bears and other toys for them. So I scour garage sales throughout the year and have donated some 100 teddy bears for boys and girls. It's a good thing for a child to have a cuddly toy to carry with them. For at least the past 10 years I've made and donated gowns for newborn babies as well. Every month, except July and August, I make approximately 10 gowns, with varying appliques and simple but unique accents Along with the donated baby clothes, A make a safe, soft sock doll for the babies and toddlers. Joining the WAAC/WAC was a very good thing I did for myself and my country. Upon learning of a need for memorabilia and articles, I donated my winter uniform to the Women's Memorial Museum in Washington, D.C.

Chapter Sixteen

YOU NEVER GET OVER BEING A NURSE

Pearl L. Bach, US Army Nurse

I graduated from nurse training in the spring of 1940, put on a white uniform, a nurse's cap with black bands, and went to work in a hospital. I worked that summer on night duty in the delivery room. That did little to prepare me for my next move, however.

On December 7, 1941 I heard over a car radio that Pearl Harbor, Hawaii, had been attacked by Japanese planes. I said that same afternoon, "Now I know what I'm going to do." I signed up as a Red Cross nurse and was assigned to the Army Nurse Corps.

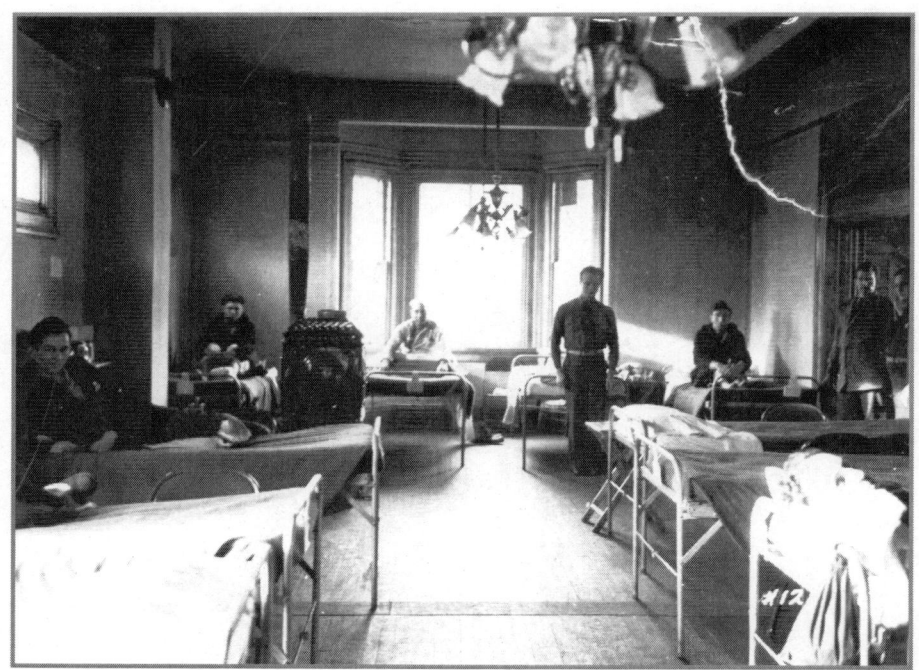

An old home in Skagway, Alaska, made into a hospital ward, Spring 1943

I entered the US Army Nurse Corps as a 2nd lieutenant at Fort Lawton, Seattle, Washington, on October 22, 1942. This was a staging area for Alaska. Here we did health evaluations and mental workups for the Army men who were being sent to the Aleutian Islands.

In April 1943 I volunteered for duty in Alaska. I was one of five RNs assigned to a small clinic and hospital in Skagway, Alaska. This clinic was for the GIs of our small transportation unit. They were sending supplies over the narrow gauge railroad to Whitehorse, Yukon Territory, for Normal Wells oil fields and for the Alcan Highway.

Three interesting incidents happened that summer. An Army RN had a "surprise" six-pound baby girl one afternoon. She had been on duty all morning. Both mother and baby were shipped back to the States in good condition. The second incident concerned our "Chief" nurse, who was a captain. She was suspected and convicted of being a morphine addict and was also shipped out. The last incident was about a new GI hospital built out in the woods east of Skagway. A staff of RN were sent up to run it, but the hospital was never used. The nurses were sent else-where. (I wonder if the hospital was just left there to rot?)

Lt. Bach (right) and fellow officer.

Christmas Eve 1943, found me on 7 p.m. to 7 a.m. night duty in a cute little hospital in Fort Nelson, British Columbia. The US Army had acquired this hospital from the Canadians, and the patient load was both Canadian and US GIs. The patients were glad to see a new face, but the Canadian nurses weren't too happy about leaving. Here again, we cared for the GIs who were helping build the Alcan Highway. It was cold there, and we lived in little log houses heated by oil. We worked and played, and I even did some skiing.

My boyfriend (I had known before either of us went into the service) had served in Panama for five years. He visited me in Edmonton, Alberta, and we decided to get married-- when we had time, that is. Late in February of 1944 I was transferred to Baxter General Hospital in Spokane for surgery. I was operated on to remove a cyst in my neck and was given a 30-day sick leave to recuperate. On April 20, 1944, I was married to T5 George W. Haugland at my parents' home in Tacoma, Washington. We spent my leave near his camp at Fort Ord, California.

I was then stationed in Vancouver, Washington, and later transferred to Fort Lewis, Washington. Here I spent some time on wards taking care of German soldier prisoners. Later that year I was put on a shipping-out list---destination

Pharmacy at Skagway, Alaska

unknown! December 20, 1944 found me and about forty other RNs on a ship headed out under the Golden Gate Bridge to who knows where. The Willard A Holbrook was a big ocean liner transformed into a troop ship. Many, many GIs were on the lower decks, and we nurses and WACs, officers and enlisted were on the upper decks. We zigged and zagged across the Pacific, and on the nineteenth day, we saw Guadalcanal off in the distance.

We were taken to New Guinea where we were given long-sleeved shirts and trousers and were allowed to become acclimated. We suffered with the heat, perspiring even while sitting still in a chair. Here we were introduced to Atabrine (which made our skin turn yellow) to prevent malaria. In about ten days we were put aboard a hospital ship and transported to Leyte, Philippine Islands. The ship was then used to transport wounded. We were put on land via a landing craft which ran up on shore.

Lt. Will (Bach) with patients at Skagway, Alaska 1943

Then we were put in the back of several GI trucks, bag and baggage. We were taken through Tacloban, where there had been fierce fighting on the original landing in October 1944. We were taken about eighteen to twenty miles back in the woods or countryside to the 133rd General Hospital. The GIs hospitalized in the big tent wards greeted us with, "You'll be sorry."

Several of the RNs who came over with us were taken at once to Manila to help liberate the nurses who had been in the Santa Tomas Prison in Manila. They were taken to another general hospital four miles from where we were. We did not see them, but we donated clothes, socks, combs, lipsticks, and other articles to these ladies, who were in pretty bad shape. The nurses' compound at 133rd General

Hospital was enclosed by a burlap fence about knee to shoulder high. A GI guard was at the gate and we had to report in and out. At first we used helmets to wash in. Later we had showers, a few stalls, outside faucets for washing and a few other conveniences.

Our tents had floors in them and tent flaps which could be put down at night. Everyone had a GI cot and special mosquito netting to tuck in during the night. Later that summer we were able to hire trusted (?) Philippine girls to do our washing and ironing. We lived out of boxes and suitcases in these tents. They were very lonesome days; it was three months before any mail came from my husband or my folks. There were other married nurses in our group, so we kind of stuck together and became friends.

Our work was caring for medical, surgical, and wounded GIs. They built more wards on our hospital. Friday, April 13, 1945, was a 24-hour day for all us nurses and others. We opened up new wards with patients who had been wounded on Samar and Sabo. They were patched up in the field hospital and sent to us. Some had grass in their casts. All were battlefield wounds. They were glad to see women and to be off of the battlefields. Most of them were treated and sent back to the States. They were being treated with this "new stuff," penicillin. The first time I ever heard of penicillin was in July 1945, while pulling night duty on a gunshot wound and fracture ward.

We did have Armed Services Radio, and I had carried my radio in a handmade case. I carried it everywhere and always with me on the ward when I was working. It was very popular with the GIs. One afternoon we heard on my radio that the US had dropped the atomic bomb on Hiroshima and later, one on Nagasaki. After that, we heard the Japanese had offered to surrender. What a day and night of celebration! Now the War would be over and we could all go home. On September 2, General McArthur accepted the Japanese surrender on board the Missouri, and a bunch of happy people listened to it over my radio.

By September 15, 1945, our hospital was closed down. Everything was inventoried, put into GI trucks and boats, taken out in the bay and dumped.

I had more than enough points for discharge but had to wait for transportation home. I waited from September 15 to November 14 without any work, just waiting and waiting. This was hard, not knowing when I would go home, and I knew my husband was discharged and waiting, too. On November 14 they took us out to a Liberty Ship in the bay. On the barge was a GI band playing "White Christmas" and "Sentimental Journey." This music still brings tears to my eyes after all these years.

It took only seven days to cross the Pacific, and we came back under the Golden Gate Bridge. On December 4, 1945, I was discharged at Camp Beale, California. Then I took a Greyhound bus to Tacoma, Washington, and the beginning of a new life.

****

Since my Army days I think my greatest contribution to life was having and raising my 4 children (2 boys and 2 girls). They are all beautiful adults now with families of their own. I worked as a hospital RN to feed my family, first at Seattle General Hospital, then at Shadle's Hospital, an alcoholic treatment center in Seattle. Then we moved to Yakima, Washington,and I worked at an osteopathic hospital for about two years.

In 1962 we moved to Hysham, Montana, and I worked for a small hospital in Forsyth, driving about 30 miles each way for 11 years. During those years and after I retired, I worked as a county nurse, school nurse, and a migrant worker's school nurse. I had a little health office in our town of Hysham.

I gave up my RN license when I turned 80 years old, but "You never get over being a nurse." I will be 90 years old on November 3, 2004.

**This writing is taken directly from "Pearl's World" written by Pearl L. Bach in December 1999, with permission of the author for use exclusively in IT'S HARD TO SALUTE STANDING IN A WALL LOCKER.

ACKNOWLEDGEMENTS

The sixteen ladies who volunteered to share their World War II memories of life in uniform, who dug into their scrapbooks and family albums for the illustrative pictures, are those to whom I will be forever grateful. They gave tangibility to my dream to record the female side of the military during those years. That is the door I wanted opened into history, and it has been cracked a wee bit by these able writers. I thank them for that.

The ladies who have told their stories, are living in Oregon, California, Montana, Ohio, Illinois, Minnesota, New Jersey, North Carolina, Virginia and Florida. They have answered from family homes, assisted living facilities, apartments, "village" parks, and even a Veterans Home. A number of them married fellows they met in the service, husbands who have passed on, leaving the ladies widowed but still brightly full of these memories they are sharing.

Each writer has become a special telephone friend of mine who I will never get to meet face-to-face. However, their interaction with me in preparing this book has sealed each one into my friendship circle.

Next-equal in importance, though in another capacity - is my computer/designer whiz and dear friend Dhyana Kearly who has given tangible form to this collection of writings. She has been politely long-suffering as she has counseled my computer ignorance, complied with last-minute changes, dealt deftly with format shifts, additions and subtractions. I so respect her advice in every area, that I know in my heart she could have taken over at any point and have given this special book its due honor. Truly, none of us ladies would have found ourselves in print without her. I am grateful to Dhyana for her patience and willingness to share her talents so graciously.

Ron Raasch, an artist with rare multi-medium skills, has honored me with his line drawing on the front cover which illustrates with panache the title of the book. As you can readily see, panache was a missing element in the event being illustrated! Thanks to Ron for lending his talent to this project.

Appropriately near the finish line, Pat Lee, a retired language arts teacher, lent her time and expertise to proof reading for spelling and mechanics. Because each contributing writer was encouraged to tell her memories "in her own words," diction and construction were a proof reader's challenge. Pat met the challenge well, and with my sincere appreciation.

One " long-sufferer" not to go unmentioned is my husband Bob who stopped just short of organizing a search and rescue team on a couple of occasions when I failed to emerge from the book-building room for hours on end. He was concerned that I would evolve into *brainruptcy* considering the intensity of my focus on this project. I need to say thank you to him for allowing that focus to go on, uninterrupted, day after day. And to just understand how important the endeavor has been to me. He has given me heart.

And to all you who read our stories, may you enjoy, recall, and/or learn.

NOTICE

The Women's Memorial

Editor's Update 2018

When this book came out in 2005, the ladies telling their personal stories about their time in the military during WWII, were in their seventies and eighties. They were recording history – 'how it really was' as pioneers in each respective branch of the service. I changed not a word of any story.

I did sense that since time marches on, someday these stories might be a legacy, that the tellers would be gone. And that is what has happened. According to my records, all have either passed, or have fallen out of contact.

In the process of making this book, I had active contact with each writer by phone and by mail. I continued touching base with them every spring, on through 2015. By then, however, so many had passed that I would go to the phone each time with a heavy heart and dreading the sound of "This number is no longer in use." Were I more computer smart, I could probably ferret out the demise and date for each lady. However, being of the same generation, I have decided to let the record stand as is. Each annotation shows as I received it, or searched it. The one exception is Marcine Richmond, SPAR, who sent me a Christmas card in 2017, but has once again fallen out of contact.

I am satisfied that these stories have been preserved. And I am equally proud to be able to claim their preservation.

May the generations to come know that patriotism is timeless. And that it is an honor to serve our country.

Peggy Lutz